OUT OF THE LION'S DEN

By
Susan Mattern

Copyright 2016 Susan Mattern

Mr. David Wade, a wildlife artist, painted the cover picture. I was able to use it courtesy of Outdoor Life Magazine.

This is a heartfelt true story of a mother's quest for truth in the wake of a tragic mountain lion attack on her young daughter. Susan Mattern genuinely recounts her search for answers in court and her search for ultimate truth in her heart. If you've never questioned your faith, this book is a splendid guide as you look through the eyes of a family's pain and hope. If you've already experienced moments of doubt, then this book is a kindred spirit that beckons you to share the journey. It is a powerful story that will help focus your own fears and doubts, and compel you to reflect on the meaning of choices, values, happenstance, and life itself.

Paul J. Levesque, Professor of Religious Studies, California State University Fullerton

To Laura

Prologue

August, 1991

The courtroom was packed with reporters, setting up video cameras and equipment along the back wall. They knew a verdict had been reached. Don slid in next to me and held my hand. We watched the schoolroom clock on the pale green wall skitter ahead, four minutes at a time, while we waited for a late juror. Finally, he ran across the tile floor, out of breath, his heels echoing on the floor like little gunshots.

The foreman handed the judge the verdict. I held my breath. Then I let it out. Nothing was happening. In the movies the verdict is one piece of paper. This verdict looked like a book.

As if in slow motion, the judge put on his glasses and started reading. He picked up a pen, held it for a few seconds, then bent over slightly and started to write. He turned the first page. My stomach churned. I clenched Don's hand tightly.

The judge wasn't smiling. I had seen his face light up with his wide smile a thousand times during the trial. He turned the second page, his face impassive. Oh God, we must have lost the case. The judge wasn't on our side, but I hoped he'd at least be pleased if we won.

The last five years swirled before me like a kaleidoscope. The mountain lion, five years of emergency rooms, endless operations, therapy, tears, screaming at an absent God, my family and their constant love, and always the mountain lion. All the images swirled back to that day when everything changed, that perfect spring day.

Chapter 1

Laura and David at Casper's Park

Palm Sunday, March 23, 1986

My five-year-old daughter Laura and I are standing in the little stream at Casper's Park. Crystal water curls around our ankles and dances gently downstream. Laura squeals in delight as a brown minnow darts past her tiny feet, then picks up a shiny pebble to show me.

"This one's pretty," she tells me.

I take the smooth green stone and put it in my shirt pocket with some black seeds. We'll add it to her collection.

Laura looks up at me with her perfectly round face and bright blue eyes. "When are they coming back?"

My husband Don and nine-year old son David have been gone a few minutes. Don, the scientist, always has to find out what's over the next hill.

"They'll be back soon." I take her hand and point downstream. "See, it looks like diamonds on the water."

We both look to where the sun lights the water with a thousand white jewels. Then the stream turns and disappears under the huge live oak trees, their gnarled branches hovering ghostlike over the dark water. I turn back to Laura, standing in the sun, her hair golden.

This March afternoon is Southern California at its best. We come to this park often. It's only about ten minutes from the coastal town of San Juan Capistrano, and about twenty minutes from our house. The rain a few days ago filled the stream and washed the sky to a deep blue. A hint of lime green covers the hills, and orange poppies dot the hillsides by the thousands, shimmering in the slight breeze.

Laura's hand wiggles out of mine. "Can I look for tadpoles now?" She takes a step away from me and bends over the water. Her straight blond hair covers her face as she looks down. She won't be distracted by anything.

Over the whisper of the water, I hear the chirping birds and the low hum of a thousand insects. An odd rustling sound makes me turn, and out of the corner of my eye, I see a large tan dog running directly at Laura. I see the muscles rippling as it runs, the short round ears, the huge velvet paws.

By the time I realize it's a mountain lion, the creature has reached Laura and grabbed her by the head. Even as my hand reaches out, even as I stumble towards her, I know I'm too late.

I'm standing alone in the stream listening to the splashing of the water. Where's Laura? She was just here a minute ago. I glance around. The birds are quiet and the hum of the insects has stopped, like a radio turned off. The overwhelming silence presses down on me. Something has happened.

The sun is warm on my back. Laura is gone. I don't know where she is. I look to the bank where she was just standing and she isn't there. The silence is loud, and then I remember the mountain lion. The tawny body, huge and muscular, slid silently towards her. The enormous jaws reached for her head. That's my last memory. I scream for help.

The trees sway above my head. Leaning over in the stream, taking huge gulps of air, the sound of my own screams is horrible in my ears. Words spill out, but I don't know what they are.

My feet can't move out of the shallow water. I bend over for more air. I'm going to faint. Laura, my daughter, my little girl, is gone, and I don't know where she is. I choke, a sickening taste in my mouth. She is gone, forever, taken away by a huge mountain lion.

Don appears in front of me, his face red from running and panic in his eyes.

"A mountain lion took Laura! I don't know where she is!"

Don turns and runs back down the trail. Why is he going away? I need him to find her, and now he's gone again. I see the red plaid of his shirt disappearing behind the trees. I don't know why he's running away.

The water splashes around my ankles as I look around aimlessly. Laura is gone, and her little white sandals lie neatly together on the bank.

The sandals lure me toward the sandy bank. I walk slowly toward them, the pebbles hard under my feet, and step out of the stream. The air feels heavy and strange, like something terrible is about to happen. But the day is still beautiful, the diamonds sparkling, the sun shining.

Nothing has happened. This is a dream, and I'm about to wake up. Waking up is hard, but I have to try. My arm and hand look so real in front of me. I can touch them. This is a terrible dream. I have to be patient, and it'll stop soon.

My brown loafers are thrown on the bank. I need to put them on, in case we go somewhere. My feet are wet. I look for a towel, but there isn't one. I slip my wet feet into the shoes.

I have no idea what to do now. The plastic container for the tadpoles is on the sand. I leave it. My camera is sitting on an old tree stump. I might need it. I don't remember why.

I reach down and pick it up by the body, not the strap. The strap goes carefully over my head so it won't accidentally drop. I'm always dropping the camera. How silly of me.

We need to go somewhere, but I can't remember where. The strawberry stand. I remember now. We're going to stop there on the way home. We're going to have strawberry shortcake for dessert tonight. Where are Don and David? And Laura?

A slight moan makes me turn. Laura. I run toward the sound, struggling through cactus and manzanita, pushing them aside.

I can't get through. The spines grab my arms and tear at my hands. I push them away. The thorns slice at my bare legs. I don't hear the moaning anymore. Stopping and listening doesn't help. Maybe a little further. A huge clump of cactus is ahead of me. I can't get around it. My arms just push through it, and I stumble and stop.

The lion is in front of me like a statue, motionless. It holds Laura by the back of her neck, and she hangs from its mouth like a rag doll.

My hands could reach out and touch the fur.

The lion watches me with blank, horrible eyes.

I don't know what to do. If I move closer, it'll run away with her, and she'll be lost again, forever this time. I scream. The sound seems distant, but I can feel my body screaming. The lion's ears flick in annoyance as I stare helplessly into its cold eyes. They have nothing in them but emptiness.

We watch each other.

The lion's massive body sits silently on the ground. I can see the individual hairs, dirty and matted. My screams don't affect it at all. The huge paws rest firmly on the ground, on each side of Laura's body. It has no fear.

Laura's hair is covered with blood, and I can't see her face. Her arms fall limply at her sides and her small hands scrape the dusty ground. Her blue flowered blouse is stained with bright crimson, and the dripping blood pools underneath her head.

The lion watches me.

I hear a sound behind me. A man stumbles up, and when he sees the lion and Laura, he stops, terror in his eyes.

He stands motionless for a second. "I'll be back. I have to get a gun." He runs away.

My sudden flicker of hope fades as he disappears from the edge of my sight. I scream again. It's all I can do. I try to think, but it's like slogging through mud. One thought comes to me. If I try to reach out to Laura, the mountain lion will turn and run away with her. I'll never see her again. I can't let that happen.

A man brushes past me. He says nothing, but pulls off a red manzanita branch, and walks slowly toward the lion. I'm there watching, but then everything goes blank. I don't see anything. I don't remember anything.

"Pick up your baby and get out of here."

Waking up suddenly, I realize the thin man is talking to me, and the lion is gone. Laura lies limp on the hard ground. I run to her, motionless in a pool of blood, kneel, and gently pick her up from the reddening dirt. I think she's dead. She isn't moving.

I can't look at her face, but I hurriedly put my hands behind her back and head, and hold her over my shoulder like I did when she was a baby. There's blood dripping everywhere.

Turning quickly, I run toward the stream. I don't know where I'm going.

Don runs up just as I reach the stream. He looks frightened, and that scares me. His face is red and puffy. He pulls off his red plaid jacket and wraps it around her head.

"Hold her down like this," he says, and I know somehow that he's right. He always knows what to do. I cradle her in my arms. Now everything will be all right, I think with a glimmer of hope. Then I realize, with an excruciating blackness, that nothing will ever be all right again. Don doesn't know yet what I know, that Laura is dead in my arms. I've seen the blood.

Don leads the way, and I run across the stream, holding Laura.

"Where's David?" I panic.

"He's with that man." Don is panting as he waits for me.

I can't think. I'm running as fast as I can. Laura is heavy in my arms, but we have to get help. I put one foot in front of the other. It's getting harder to run as the ground slopes upward.

Green grass and wildflowers blur by my side. Loose pebbles slip under my wet shoes. The trail widens into a dirt road. I have to stop, out of breath, just for a second.

Laura's arm hangs limply. I see her little motionless hand that I was holding just a few minutes ago. I can't see her face. It's covered with Don's red plaid jacket.

Don stops and turns back to me and takes Laura carefully from my arms. He looks so frightened, but he can't be. He knows how to solve every problem.

I try to keep up with him. It's easier running without Laura. I glance at my watch. It looks unfamiliar to me, a silly watch I bought at the grocery store for five dollars. It has a picture of a Disney witch on it. Laura thought it was funny.

Two o'clock in the afternoon. My friend Linda is just getting home from church. I need to call her. Maybe she can help. I don't know why I'm thinking this. It's such a strange thought. Maybe if we can get past these trees and campgrounds and back to the picnic area, then everything will be better. I can't think about Laura dying.

People are in the picnic area, under huge live oak trees next to red and yellow tents. Smoke curls from barbeques. I hear faraway laughter. Why are they having fun? Laura isn't moving at all. It seems cruel that other people are laughing. Everything seems so very far away.

Don screams at them, "There's a mountain lion. Get out of here!" No one moves. They don't hear him.

Pebbles and rocks slip under my shoes. The sun is getting hotter. Don stops, breathing heavily. I take Laura from him and start running again.

"Somebody help us," I try to scream, but my voice is a whisper. I think this road ends in a dirt parking lot. It must be close with all the people and picnic tables we've seen.

I can't think about my daughter dying in my arms.

Linda will be getting home and I'll find a telephone and tell her what happened. I can't think about Laura right now. Just focus on the trail.

The lion is in my eyes, staring at me.

How can I live without Laura? I push the thought away.

The gravel road goes up a hill. I can't go any further, but I have to. With a last burst of energy, I start to run.

As we reach the crest of the hill, the green bushes and grass blurring beside us, a man appears in front of me, arms outstretched.

It's the thin man who fought off the lion. He's taking Laura from me, and I'm just handing my daughter to a complete stranger. But he's the man who saved her. I let go of Laura.

Don is next to me, bending over, out of breath.

The man turns with Laura, and runs quickly down the hill. A green ranger truck is waiting at the bottom of the road, past the long rope chains, its engine running. We reach the end of the road. It must be there for Laura. Someone got help for us. A man with a ranger hat sits behind the wheel. His worried expression frightens me. The man holding Laura puts her gently on the vinyl front seat, jumps in the back, and the truck starts to move.

"Wait! We're her parents!" I stumble down the hill in a panic. They can't leave without us.

The truck stops and Don climbs in the back. David is sitting in the back, and I open the cab door and slide on the seat next to Laura.

She is propped up next to the ranger, her head slumped over in an odd position, like a broken doll, not moving at all. I don't dare move her.

There is blood everywhere. The ranger looks at me as I try to hold her steady, and, in a reassuring voice, he says. "She'll be all right."

He's lying, just trying to make me feel better.

The truck bounces on the dirt road. I feel it jump up on the sudden paved road, and the ride is smoother. My arms hold Laura, so she won't fall over on the seat. I think she might be breathing. I can't tell. We drive faster, leaning into the curves. The walkie-talkie sputters mechanical sounds that make no sense, but the ranger answers and says we're on our way. I don't know where.

The truck pulls up to the visitor center. A ranger runs around and takes Laura carefully from the seat, Don's jacket still covering her head. I follow them into a small windowless room. The walls are white, with a cot by the wall and a stand with bandages and a bottle of hydrogen peroxide. There must be more medical supplies but I don't see anything.

The little room is crowded. A ranger asks me to stand outside so I walk out the door. He looks worried. I don't think he knows what to do.

Don and David are standing by the white wall. The three of us stand there, waiting, not together, but each of us alone on that concrete walkway.

The lion looms in front of me. I can't get it out of my eyes. It replays over and over, like a video, that same scene. The lion looks blankly into my eyes.

I hear a siren. It must be for Laura. I lean against the white concrete wall, hoping that someone can help her. I want to be with her, but the two rangers are inside and there's no more room. My shaking hands are covered with blood.

The ambulance stops directly in front of me. Two paramedics jump out. There's a moment of confusion, and then a ranger leads them into the small room. I want to be with her. I walk to the doorway, but a ranger stops me. The room is too crowded. This is my daughter, I plead with him silently. But I stay outside.

When I close my eyes, the lion races toward Laura. When I open my eyes, it stares at me.

A man comes up and throws a glass of water in my face. I think he's trying to wash the blood off my face, but I don't even ask him why. He's the man who wanted to get the gun. He stands, talking with a woman. I can't hear anything they're saying.

I can't stand up anymore. My body sinks down on the concrete walk, and my hands feel the warm sidewalk. I close my eyes tightly in an attempt to shut everything out, but the attack replays in my mind.

Laura has to be alive or they would tell us. Why are they waiting so long to get help? There's nothing in that room to help her. She needs to be in a hospital. She needs to go in the ambulance. I don't understand.

Don walks up to a ranger. I can't hear what they're saying, but Don comes over to me and says they're waiting for a helicopter. Why isn't it here? I look at my watch. When we ran down the trail it was two o'clock and now it's almost three. I can distinguish some words from the muffled sounds coming from the room: "helicopter," "San Juan Capistrano," "Swallows Day." At last a ranger comes out and talks to Don. I get up awkwardly and walk over to them.

"We're trying to get a helicopter. It's only three minutes by helicopter to Mission Hospital. We don't want to take the ambulance because we're worried about the freeway traffic. It's Swallow's Day at the mission."

Tears come to my eyes. No matter how bad the traffic was, they could have been at the hospital by now. But I have to put my trust in these people. I hope the helicopter comes soon. I feel helpless.

The man who saved Laura, thin and slightly built, is sitting on the grass talking to David. He was so brave to go in there with the branch. I have no idea what he did. He somehow drove off the lion and saved Laura.

I have betrayed my daughter. The thought washes coldly over me. I should have been the one who saved her. Instead, I stood by stupidly and watched someone else rescue her. When the test came, I failed.

A bitter taste fills my mouth. I want her to live so much. How can she live, with all the blood she's lost?

Suddenly everyone is moving. The helicopter is coming and will land in a field down the road. The paramedics carry Laura to the ambulance, and I run to her side. The paramedic nods and I climb up the back step. Don and David get in the ranger truck.

Laura's head is covered with a towel, but blood seeps new and crimson onto the white cloth. Between the paramedics, I see just a glimpse of her on the stretcher in the cramped ambulance. I hold on to a strap from the ceiling as we swerve around curves.

I'm the first to climb out. We're next to a large field of waist-high wildflowers and poppies. Don and David come up next to me. My son will be so excited to see the helicopter. He loves airplanes and even though he's only nine, he knows the name of every fighter jet in the world. Then I remember that Laura is dying.

I lean on Don and put my arm around David. What looks like a brown toy comes over the blue mountain ridge, growing larger every second. Hovering over the field, the blurred blades whip the tall brown grass into waves.

A fireman stands by in case the field catches fire. The helicopter sets down gently on the grass, and the individual blades slow to a stop. One of the paramedics runs toward the helicopter and climbs inside. The other takes Laura and runs by us, not stopping, to the open helicopter door. I reach out to Laura, and again I'm too late.

Don grabs a ranger's arm and asks if we can go, but there's only room for the pilot and the paramedic holding Laura. I grab Don's hand, resting on David's back. The brown grass flattens in waves as the helicopter blades spin slowly, then blur. The helicopter wobbles as it slowly rises, then hangs motionless in the air before it moves away, gathering speed. I watch till it disappears beyond the hills.

The grass is motionless and I strain to hear a sound, but there's only silence. A policeman walks toward us, his shoes crunching the gravel path, and asks if we want to ride with him to the hospital. I look at the empty sky and slide in the back seat of his patrol car.

The police car retraces our happy ride of a few hours ago. We reach the park entrance and slow down for a speed bump. There are cars lined up at the entrance, waiting to go in the park. The ranger is motioning for them to turn away. He sees us and waves us on like he's in control of the police car.

I lean against the window and watch as the trees slip by. How ugly they are. The oak trees reach over the road, their branches overgrown and brown, hiding a thin layer of new green leaves. Dead grass whips by, and the faraway hills slip in and out of my vision. Trees blur beside the road. I hate this road. I promise myself that I'll never go down it again.

I look at my bare white legs and try to pull out some of the cactus spines. There are hundreds of them. I don't remember going through that much cactus. It's terrible that I'm thinking about myself. But I don't want to think about Laura.

We're on the freeway now, and the siren is loud in my ears. We pull to the center divider and pass all the cars. It feels odd to be in a police car. I remember why we're in it and where we're going. I pray that Laura is still alive. Just a few hours ago we drove down this same freeway, laughing and joking about the day, hoping to catch some tadpoles for David's science experiment at school. Now I look out the window and catch sight of those perfect clouds in the blue sky. Nothing will ever be the same again.

Chapter 2

Laura two days before attack

Sunday, March 23, Mission Hospital

As we speed down the freeway, I ask God to save her life. I don't care what's wrong with her, just so she lives. I know He can do anything. I've been a Catholic all my life, a nun for six years, and leaving the convent hasn't lessened my belief in God's power.

I wonder suddenly why God let this happen. She's only five-years old. She's never done anything wrong. And there are so many other children who get hurt and die. I never wondered why. Of course I know all about good and evil and why bad things happen to people. But right now, I just can't think of any possible reason why God would let this happen.

We pull off the freeway and into the emergency entrance of Mission Hospital. We get out and stand unsure on the curb. David stares longingly at the helicopter just a few feet away, where the pilot has his hand on the helicopter door, talking to the paramedic. He waves to us in recognition. David quickly waves back. The policeman leads us through the automatic doors.

We want to see Laura, but a volunteer takes us down the long green corridor to a small waiting room. I look back. The policeman is looking down at the black and white linoleum floor.

Don and I sit on the hard vinyl chairs. David sits between us, his mud-splattered legs swinging back and forth in his big tennis shoes. One shoe is untied. I close my eyes. I see the lion and open them quickly.

I stare at my bare legs and pick out more cactus spines. A generic picture of a washed-out forest hangs tilted on the far wall.

A distinguished man in a white lab coat walks in. "I'm Dr. Michael Kennedy, head of the trauma team. We'll be taking your daughter into surgery soon. We have a neurosurgeon, a plastic surgeon, and an ophthalmologist on our team, and we'll try to keep you informed of everything that's happening."

He quickly shakes our hands and walks out of the room. I sit down again.

In the silence, David looks up at me and says, "Mom, I think she's going to be all right." I hold his hand tight. For some reason, David's nine-year old confidence makes me feel better. He's such a good son. We sit quietly for a few minutes. I want to call my friend Linda. I keep thinking that she can help, although I don't know how.

"Don," I touch his shoulder, "I'm going to call Linda." He nods, and then stares straight ahead. I walk outside the door, spot a volunteer and ask for a telephone. She points to the lobby and hurries on.

I know Linda's number by heart. I think back to this morning's Palm Sunday services. Laura sat on the piano bench with me while I played. I was so afraid she would accidently touch the keyboard that I sent her down to sit with David in the congregation. Afterwards, I bought some Easter eggs for them outside the church. I desperately want to be back there, this morning, when life was still good.

"Hi." Linda's cheerful voice answers.

"Linda?" My voice catches.

"What's wrong?"

"It's Laura. She got attacked by a mountain lion. We're down at Mission Hospital and she's going into surgery."

"What!"

"I don't know if she's going to live." I finish quickly, not daring to say more as my throat tightens.

"Oh my God. I'll be down as soon as I can."

I hang up the phone, and sit for a minute in the busy lobby. There, that was simple to say. I feel like a character in a play, reciting my lines. Nothing seems real. I shake my head, trying to clear it, and walk back to the waiting room.

Another doctor walks in. He's tall with tightly curled brown hair. He has a kind look about him.

"I'm Doctor Weiss, a pediatric ophthalmologist. I'll be checking your daughter's eye during surgery. The pressure in her right eye is low, and we need to find out why."

As he shakes my hand, he looks at me with such a sad expression, I want to tell him that everything will be fine, and then I remember, it's Laura's life that hangs in the balance.

We sit in silence. David looks through magazines. Don stares straight ahead, not saying anything. For once, I'm glad not to talk. What can be said? Laura is dying. No one can lose that amount of blood and still live. I see the lion, no matter where I look in the room. I can't wipe it off my mind. I want to tear it out of my eyes.

Linda appears at the door with her husband Joe. She's still dressed for church, her short black hair neatly framing her thin face. I stand up and we hug as she cries for me. My best friend will help me, even though I don't know how.

The policeman from the park asks Don about our car. The car. It's still at the park. I had forgotten all about it. I don't ever want to see that park again. I hate it. Don goes with him, while Linda and I sit in the waiting room.

"Do you want to tell me what happened?"

I start to tell the story. I don't cry or feel any emotion at all, because it's a story, just a story. I can't connect it with what just happened to us.

Linda cries, but my eyes are dry. I see the lion every time I close them.

I look up at the clock every few minutes, wondering when the surgery will begin. It's been over two hours. Don comes back from the park, looking pale and sick.

"Have you heard anything?"

"No, nothing."

He stands in front of me, uncertain.

"I need to tell you something. Come out here with me."

We walk out in the corridor. "I got the car. But when I was down there, the ranger said something really strange. He said, 'I'm sorry about your daughter. I hope she'll be all right.' Then he said, 'We've been having a lot of trouble with that mountain lion lately.'"

I look at Don, trying to understand. It comes to me in a rush.

"They knew the lion was there? And they didn't say anything?"

"That's what the ranger said. I must have looked shocked, because he stopped then and didn't say anything else. I have a feeling he wasn't supposed to tell me that." Don shakes his head.

"We even asked if everything was ok." I'm trying to make sense of it.

I think back to when we drove into the park. It had rained a lot in the last few weeks, so Don asked the ranger about the roads.

"Is there anything else we need to know?" Don asked, always careful. The ranger looked up at the long line of cars behind us. "No, have a nice day."

Don and I stand silently for a minute. I don't even have the emotional energy to give him a hug. I touch his arm. His face, usually serious, looks like a mask has been pulled over it. We walk back in the waiting room. I can't think about the ranger right now.

A woman in a pin-striped suit walks briskly into the room. "I'm sorry to bother you, but we had a phone call from the *Los Angeles Times*. They'd like to talk to you about your daughter. If you want, you can use the phone in the lobby." She hands me a small piece of yellow paper with a phone number, turns and leaves the room.

"How did they find out about Laura?" I whisper to Don.

Don looks at me from far away. "They have to file a police report. And the call went out for the ambulance and helicopter."

Of course they would know by now.

I clench the little yellow paper. "Do you want to talk to them?"

He looks up at me, his face empty. "Why don't you do it?"

I sit back in the uncomfortable chair. I don't want to talk to anyone. Then I think about our friends. My mom and dad! I have to call them. They love her so much. I have to call them and let them know.

Don looks up at me. "Maybe it would be good to talk to the paper. To get the story right."

I wander out to the phone in the lobby and make the call. The reporter thanks me and wants to know every detail. I'm not used to so many questions. He assures me that the article will be in the morning's paper and asks if I have a picture of Laura. No, and I'm not going home to get a picture. My place is here. Home seems very far away. He hopes Laura will be fine and we hang up.

I have to call my mom and dad. They live in St. Louis and they're in their seventies, too old for news like this. I put my hand on the phone but I can't pick it up. If I tell them about Laura, it will be real. It'll go on and on and last forever.

My mom is the official worrier for the whole family. She reminds us about snakes when we go hiking, and worries about car accidents, train wrecks, cancer, and seat belts. Don and I just laugh at most of her warnings, not to her face, of course. I don't want to live my life being afraid. Maybe mom was right. We had plenty to worry about. We just didn't know it.

There is still a part of me that doesn't believe this has happened. I'll call my sister Carol. She'll know what to do. I dial my sister's number.

The connection is bad and she can't hear me very well. I talk louder and repeat that it was a mountain lion. She can't believe what I'm telling her. Why would she? I can barely believe it. She wants to fly out right away but I want her to tell Mom and Dad. I promise to call as soon as Laura gets out of surgery. Carol decides that she and Jane, my other sister, will go down and tell Mom and Dad. They'll be waiting for my call.

I hang up. My eyes are dry. When I get back to the waiting room, our pediatrician, Dr. Shannon, is there. I feel better knowing that he's come to help. He's wearing his usual jeans and cowboy boots, and a plaid shirt with all the trimmings. David stands up shyly and says hello. Dr. Shannon gives us all a hug and says he'll be in surgery with the trauma team. His presence fills the room and when he leaves, everyone is quiet again.

Sunday evening, March 23

A volunteer tells us Laura has been taken into surgery and escorts us down the hall to a different waiting room. The time is 5 pm. I sit with nothing in my hands. My purse has been lost somewhere.

The minutes tick by slowly. No one says anything. A dark smudge on the wall bothers me. I want to get up and wash it off. I don't want to think about anything else.

Linda's voice startles me. "Maybe we should go to the restroom and you can clean up a little." I look at my hands and clothes with the bloodstains on them. I'm embarrassed that she had to mention it, and then I don't really care.

We walk to a restroom. I lean over the sink, lit by cold fluorescent lights, and stare in the mirror. The lights make me look old and tired. I'm thirty-six years old and look like I'm fifty. My shoulder-length brown hair hangs limply. I look pale without any makeup. My thin wire glasses reflect the bright lights above me.

I use wet brown paper towels to wash my face and hands, but the towels fall apart. I try washing my legs, but cactus spines are still in them and I stop. My blouse is red and white checkered and I realize a lot of the red is blood. I have to go home and take care of things like clothes and the house and getting cleaned up, but nothing matters right now except Laura. I stare at the mirror. I've run out of things to do. Everything is closing in on me. Linda asks if I'm finished and we walk back to the waiting room.

I look at the clock. Almost eight o'clock. Laura's been in surgery for three hours. I wonder how much longer it's going to take. A young man in blue scrubs walks in. "Mr. Small?" he says to the room. Don and I stand up and follow him into the hall. He's younger than I am, handsome with curly black hair, probably a medical assistant.

"I'm Dr. Sylvain Palmer, the neurosurgeon on the trauma team. I'll be honest. Laura's head injuries are the worst I've ever seen. We're going to do our best. We've only started to get out bone shards that have penetrated the brain. I want you to be prepared because it's going to take a long time."

I manage to get back to my chair and close my eyes. *The worst head injury I've ever seen.* The words keep spinning through my head. The doctor seems so young; maybe he hasn't seen many head injuries. *The worst head injury.* Think of something else. Anything. Palm Sunday. The long reading of the Passion. I always hate that reading. I think of Laura's blood, and the tearing of her scalp, like the crown of thorns. Christ died to save the world. But where's the meaning in her suffering? What possible reason could God have to make her suffer and die?

Right before we took our vows in the convent, we had to make a crown of thorns and put it in a decorated wooden box. The crown was supposed to be meaningful, something about Christ's suffering, or our sacrifice to serve him, or some message that I apparently missed. Most of my class took it as a joke, a show and tell, and decorated our boxes with flowers and bright colors. What a silly fake thing, made by teenagers who had never suffered anything in our whole lives. Laura's crown of thorns is real.

I start making deals with God, desperate to make Him real to me.

"If you let her live, I'll do anything for you. I'll never doubt again. I'll believe in you forever." Laura's life is in God's hands, so I have to be careful. What if I don't really believe strongly enough and he lets her die? God wouldn't do that, I tell myself quickly. But he let her get attacked by a mountain lion. I'm confused, but try to push away all my doubts for Laura's sake.

Why is this happening to us? We're good parents. The kids are never out of my sight. We wear seat belts and I would never have a gun in the house. I don't even let Laura play alone out in the front yard.

David is swinging his legs next to me. I put my hand on his arm, glad he's there with us, and he looks up from a magazine. Suddenly, I think of the little boy down the street. What's his name? His mother lets him run wild. I've seen cars swerve to miss him. He comes up to our house to play, but Laura doesn't like him, and I don't want her playing with him. I'm too careful with Laura. And now he's fine and Laura is dying. What did I do wrong? Finally, my eyes sting with tears.

Dr. Weiss walks in and sits next to us.

"The back of your daughter's eye was badly torn. That's why the pressure was low. I've repaired it, but only time will tell if the surgery's a success."

"How did it get torn?"

"The tooth of the mountain lion must have torn the back of the eye." He shakes his head. He leaves the room, but leaves me with that horrible image.

Maybe God is punishing me for leaving the convent. What a stupid thought. I quickly dismiss it. My God is kind and loving, not cruel. Then why did He let this happen? If He is all-powerful, He could have prevented this. It would have been simple for Him. Maybe God isn't who I think He is.

I had joined the convent to discover God. Ever since I was little, I had wondered about what God was like. By my senior year, the church was changing-a new pope, an ecumenical spirit, social activism, and finally, rights for women. The convent seemed like the Peace Corps, only better.

I remember that first day in the convent, full of anticipation. An old brass school bell rang out across the green lawns overlooking the Mississippi River. The August sun beat down on my family as we said our final goodbyes and gave hugs all around. I loved my mom and dad and sisters, although hugs were unusual. Political discussions were more the norm. Clutching my small suitcase, I waved goodbye as I stepped through the towering wooden doors. The doors closed slowly, blocking out the light as my eyes tried to adjust to the sudden darkness.

In all the six years I was in the convent, I never discovered God.

I move around in the vinyl chair, trying to find a comfortable position. I see the lion when I close my eyes, so I open them and stare at the clock. The second hand sputters its way around the face and when I look up only five minutes has passed.

I lean over to pick up a magazine. Hair and nail ads and movie stars splash across the pages. I throw the magazine down and lean back against the green wall, feeling sick.

Don's eyes are closed. I wonder, as usual, what he's thinking. He's only thirty-nine, but he looks old and tired. His round face has lines I've never noticed. There are a few grey hairs in his beard and moustache. He is always hard to read and has often been depressed. Now he's even further away and we sit silently across the wide room.

Linda's husband offers to take David to stay with their two boys. David's restless, sitting with us for hours. He's worried about Laura but he's only nine. Don and I hug David tightly before he goes. I know he'll be fine.

Linda touches my arm. "Do you want to go outside for a while?" I think the fresh air will help. I look at

Don. He's sitting silently, staring at the wall. I can't even worry about what he's feeling. I can barely feel anything. I put my hand on his shoulder. He looks up at me, startled, and I tell him about going outside. He barely nods.

Linda and I walk down the dimly lit corridors and out the front door. I lean on a rusted railing wet with dew. The parking lot is desolate and lonely, a darkness spreading out to the road beyond. The night sky is a dark blue with pinpoints of stars. The moon has risen over the horizon but the light barely illuminates the darkness.

"I don't understand why God lets things like this happen," I say out loud to the night.

Linda shakes her head sadly. "I don't know. I asked myself that when my sister died, and when Becky's husband died in the helicopter crash. But I think there's a reason, even though we don't know what it is right now."

It's true, I suddenly realize, as guilt washes over me, that all these people I know and work with have troubles of their own. I never talked to our fellow choir member Becky about her husband's death, only a few short years ago. They were newly married and he was a Marine. I never once asked about Linda's sister. I close my eyes, realizing too much at once.

"I used to believe in God so strongly when I went in the convent," I ramble on, trying not to think about my insensitivity, "but now I just don't know what to believe anymore. I believe in God, but what kind of a

God can let horrible things happen to little children like Laura?"

"I don't know," Linda says. "I really don't know."

I watch the black sky for a few more minutes. If God will let Laura live, I'll never question Him again my whole life. I vow to do whatever he wants. I don't know what he wants. I've never known. We walk back to the waiting room.

Monday, March 24

The hospital is dark and quiet at three in the morning. I sweep down the long corridors of my life, looking in doorways dark and silent, trying to find that one moment where God was real to me. There had to be a time when I was sure of his presence, when I knew he had answered a prayer, or had spoken to me. If I can find that moment, then maybe Laura will live.

I see the blood orange sun rising over the Mississippi River so many years ago, and how I marveled that it was God's work. When I touched my baby's feather-soft face for the first time, I thanked Him for the miracle of birth. I had prayed in stained glass cathedrals, monuments to those who had felt his presence. The final chords of Bach would leave me in tears at God's beauty. Laura would run so fast into my arms, and laugh as we tumbled over on the grass.

But those were all moments when I pushed God into the picture. He wasn't really there. Why can't I find one real moment of God in my whole life? One second where he was actually present, not just in my imagination? My mind slips and falls. I can't find him anywhere.

Now I look up at our friends Cindy and Roger, sitting together across the room. Cindy, as always, is alert and ready to help. Roger leans his head back against the wall, his eyes closed. Don met Roger at work years ago, and we've known them since our boys were babies. Linda sits next to me, and Don on my other side. I want to take his hand, but he seems so far away. My family doctor and his wife, whom I barely know, sit across the room and wait with us. It's been ten hours. No one has anything to say. I want to thank them, but I don't know what to say.

A small man in green hospital scrubs walks into the room. I struggle to remember his name as he bows. Watanabe. That's it. He's the plastic surgeon. Don and I get up, my legs stiff under me.

"Laura's still in surgery, but my part is finished for now. Her skull was crushed in many places. It took over 900 stitches to close the wounds to her head and face." *Nine hundred stitches! That's impossible.* "Many tendons and nerves in the face still need to be repaired. We repaired her sinuses but there will need to be more surgeries. There is an area where there is only the dura, the membrane that covers the brain. There is no skull there to cover it." *How can she live like that? I don't understand.* "Hopefully we can put a metal plate in her skull soon, to cover that area…"

I have to sit down and Don listens to the rest of what Dr. Watanabe has to tell us.

What does Laura look like right now? They wouldn't let me see her. All I remember is Don's red flannel shirt wrapped around her head, the blood dripping. I touch my blood-stained shirt. Her blood, dried and brown.

I see Laura in my mind now, her golden hair framing her ivory face. Her face round like Don's, her lips full. She pushes her way through life, never stopping. Screams of delight or tears of anger. Nothing in between. David thinks and chooses carefully, full of quiet. Laura grabs life and shakes it. She always knows what she wants.

When I was pregnant with Laura, I wondered how my two children could be different. David was such an easy, happy child. I couldn't imagine anyone else. But Laura grabbed our lives and sent them spinning from the moment she was born. *Over nine hundred stitches. It's not possible.*

At four in the morning, Dr. Shannon, Laura's pediatrician, comes out of the surgery and asks if we want to sleep for a while.

Sleep? No, I don't want to sleep. I never want to sleep again. I manage to say out loud, "No, I want to be here when Laura comes out of surgery." Don agrees. Dr. Shannon puts his hand on my arm gently and asks me to come out to the corridor. We stand in the darkened hall, tiny fluorescent lights flickering overhead. He's sure of what he's going to say.

"You have to get some sleep. You have to be there for Laura when she gets out of surgery. Go ahead. You need to do this for her, not for yourself."

I stand awkwardly, wanting to lean against the wall. My arms feel detached. I don't know whether to fold them or let them hang. Dr. Shannon takes me down the twilight halls into a small, dark room where the doctors sleep on a hard exam bed in the middle of the room. I lie down on the unfamiliar antiseptic sheets and close my eyes, knowing I can't sleep.

All I can see is the attack, the blood, the thin man with the stick, the stream, the lion. But apparently I do sleep, because suddenly a huge mountain lion is running toward me. The eyes are blank and evil. It towers over Laura and I can't stop it. I wake up, my heart pounding. The darkness is all around me.

Chapter 3

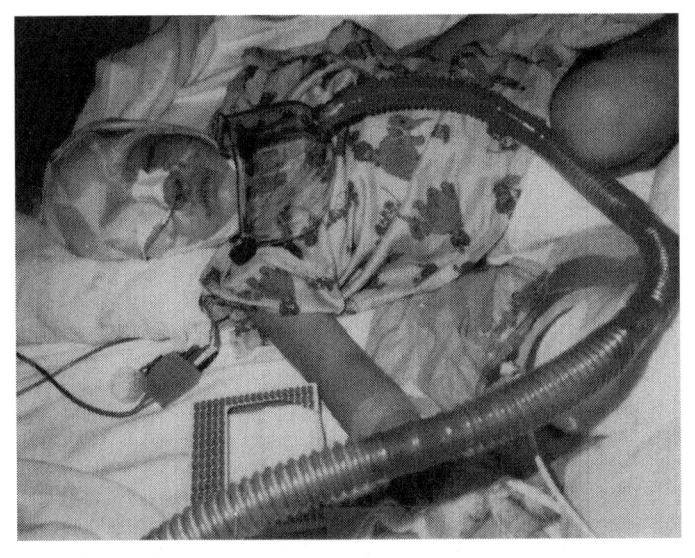

Laura in intensive care

Monday, March 24, morning

I'm freezing and pull an unfamiliar blanket up over me. Where am I? Oh, God, I remember. In the hospital. My head is groggy from the sleeping pill.

I look at my watch and can barely make out the thin lines. The room is dark, with one feeble nightlight attempting a few shadows in the corner. I sit up quickly, my head spinning. I move my arm so I can see my watch in the feeble light. Seven in the morning. That can't be right. Something went wrong with the surgery. It's been over fourteen hours. Why didn't they get me? What if Laura died, and I never got to see her? I've been forgotten. I feel like throwing up.

A knock at the door startles me. The door opens slowly and I see a figure framed in the light.

"Your daughter's coming out of surgery."

I jump up and sway unsteadily on the tile floor. She's still alive. My heart pounds rapidly. But what's happening?

There's no time to ask. I follow the volunteer down the corridor. My stomach sickens with every step. At the end of the corridor, Don is waiting. His eyes are dark circles in the harsh light. I wonder if he's slept at all. He takes my hand as we walk.

Dr. Shannon meets us outside the wide doors of the intensive care unit.

"I would stay longer," he says in his big voice, "but I've got to get to work. Laura's stabilized and we really can't do anything but wait."

I realize that Dr. Shannon has been at the hospital all night and is just now going to work. What a good person he is. We are so lucky to know him.

The automatic doors open wide, and we walk down the corridor to the last room. Machines fill the room, whirring and beeping, and nurses are walking around the bed in the center. I hold my breath. I can do this.

Don and I walk together to the bed. My fingers slip out of his hand. A white sheet outlines a small figure. It's hard to see her among the sheets and blankets. Her head is completely wrapped in bandages, except for one closed eye. The eye is red and bruised. The other eye has a patch over it. Her nose is in a cast. Two tubes come from her mouth and snake into a maze of large steel machines. Her two arms are at her side, one on a board with an IV connected to it, the other lifeless.

I'm horrified, and try to wish this all away. I want to go back to yesterday and start over. Laura looks like a random towel thrown on the white bed. There's only one tiny place on her body that isn't hooked up to wires, and I gently put my hand on her arm.

This is my daughter, my bright, blue-eyed daughter, whom I love so much. The nurse touches my arm, "Talk to her. I think she can probably hear you."

How horrible it must be to lie there, only able to hear voices, not understanding what happened. Don tells her how much we love her, and I sit down in a chair before I faint.

After a few minutes, Don wipes his eyes and leaves the room. I get up and touch her again.

"Laura, it's me, mom. You're going to be ok." I've run out of things to say. I can't say all those encouraging things other people say. I can't lie. The respirator breathes for her, steady and loud. The heart monitor beeps constantly. My words are lost among all the machines.

I touch her little hand. God could have prevented this. He has abandoned us. Laura has been thrown into the lion's den, like Daniel in the Old Testament, but

God hasn't saved her. How could he have let this happen?

This is not the time to question. This is the time to pray, to beg for her life, to promise Him anything. I push God's betrayal from my mind, but it keeps pushing back in. Maybe He's angry with me for leaving the convent. The thought is ridiculous, but it lodges in my brain like a pebble in a shoe.

I watch her breathing, the machines forcing air inside her body. Then another thought comes, uninvited, unwanted. What if God isn't mean and vengeful? What if He isn't anything at all? What if there is no God?

I can't breathe. All those years of believing slip through my mind, all those dreams, all those hopes. Were all those prayers to a vast emptiness? Is that the answer?

I push that thought as far away as I can and take a breath. Laura. She's the only thought in my mind. Please wake up and laugh again. Just yesterday she had boundless energy, and a love of fancy lace dresses. Her favorite things were unicorns, ballet, and Strawberry Shortcake movies. She passed her kindergarten readiness test just last week. I had laughed: of course Laura could run and balance on one foot.

Now I look at the bandages and wonder if she'll ever walk again. Dr. Palmer, the young neurosurgeon, said she's paralyzed on her right side. Will she speak, or know what she's saying?

The room closes in on me. The refrain of "no God" pounds in my head. This moment, as I hold her limp hand, thinking of a vast emptiness instead of a God, is the bleakest moment of my life.

Monday afternoon, March 24

Don and I divide up the days and nights, and I go home for the first time since the attack. I fumble with the car keys, and stare inside the car. A plastic container for tadpoles lies on the back seat, along with Laura's "Goodnight Moon" book and some Legos. Palm fronds are thrown in the back window from the Palm Sunday service. Was that only yesterday?

I pull out of the parking lot. It's odd to be driving again. The people on the freeway have no idea how quickly their lives could change. I want to tell them. The familiar buildings and freeway exits look different, like I've awakened from a long dream.

Our small white ranch house with green trim has been our home for 10 years, but I can't shake the sensation that I've been away for a long time.

As I walk up the sidewalk, our black cat runs out from the bushes, meowing loudly. No one came home last night and he's hungry. Suddenly I'm angry. A huge cat just tried to kill my daughter, and I kick him away, hard. Sylbuster cries and runs from me. Tears well up in my eyes. I've never acted like this before. My anger is gone now and I call to him. I kneel down in front of the bushes, but he won't come to me. I'm so sorry, my little cat. I fumble to find the right key to unlock the door.

This is my house, but I'm the stranger. I see the unimportance of our lives scattered on the living room floor. Red and white Legos, a stuffed bear of Laura's, its plump legs sticking up as if frozen on the carpet. She might not live long enough to play with it again. I banish this thought and move to the kitchen, where the answering machine blinks rapidly, seven or eight times. I turn it on.

"Sue, this is Joyce. I heard about Laura this morning. Let me know if there's anything we can do. Please call us. Anything!" Click.

"This is Robin from the *National Enquirer*. Please call me back at ——"

I turn off the machine. I can't listen. Sunday's newspaper is still scattered on the table, and the grandfather clock ticks in the silence.

"His Eye is on the Sparrow," a choir song we performed yesterday, lies on the kitchen table. I resist the urge to tear it into a thousand pieces. How can anyone think that God cares for each little sparrow, and Laura, and all the other dying people in intensive care?

Papers from Don's computer business lie in piles on the table, all meaningless.

As I look around the room, these little things seem so cheap now, like costume jewelry.

I walk hesitantly into Laura's bedroom. "My Little Pony" lies on the floor, its tiny comb stuck in its pink mane. Laura's blue flowered Easter dress lies crumpled, and picture books are scattered on the carpet. Her school picture sits on the dresser. I pick it up and sit down on her bed. As I hold it, I cry for that little girl who has been changed forever.

She has always been her own little person, so sure of herself. I realize how much I love all those little things that make her Laura. Her stubbornness, her round face, her joy of life. What if she's in some institution for the rest of her life? I pray, and make more deals with the God I just denied.

It's late afternoon when I get back to the hospital. Don gets up quickly as I walk into Laura's room. "She's the same."

He squeezes her hand and kisses her, but Laura doesn't move.

I sit for a while in Laura's room. In the coming darkness, the little high window turns from white to gray. The machines whirr, and I can hear Laura's breathing through the respirator and watch the sheet over her body move lightly up and down.

I put my hand on hers.

Dr. Shannon comes to the door, with the same Hawaiian shirt that he wore on Sunday. He hasn't even been home. He arrived at 3:00 on Sunday afternoon, stayed for Laura's entire operation through Monday morning, then went to his office and worked a full day, checked on her a few times when I was gone, and now, at 6:30 Monday night, is finally leaving.

Tears come to my eyes. I'm so grateful. I start to thank him but he shrugs his shoulders, puts his big arms around me for a second, and then leaves.

The small window turns black. I sit on the rickety cot across from Laura's bed, trying not to think. A big can of Almond Roca sits on the cot beside me, unopened, next to my brown purse-someone must have found it-and a few stuffed animals.

A nurse brings a list of phone messages. I'm overwhelmed. For the next few hours I run in and out of Laura's room to see visitors. Her pre-school teacher comes by with a gift. Ruth and Don, our elderly friends from Leisure World, and Father Steve from my parish, stop by.

Finally, visiting hours are over. I move a few things off the cot and try to sleep. Linda's in the waiting room and stays the night again. I sit with her. Then I'm afraid to be away from Laura, and I come back and sit on the cot, waiting for the black window to turn to gray.

Chapter 4

Tuesday, March 25

I don't know what day it is. I think it's Tuesday. Don comes in when the window turns gray and I go home for a few hours. I can't sleep. I make a cup of hot chocolate and eat a bowl of cereal.

I call Linda's house and talk to David.

"Are you ok there?"

"Yeah."

"What have you been doing?"

"Playing video games and stuff. Is Laura gonna be ok?"

"I hope so. I'll call you later today."

I decide to go back to the hospital. As I drive back, the green landscaping along the freeway reminds me of Casper's Park and my heart starts pounding. A car rudely pulls in front of me and tears come to my eyes. I can't remember if I brought my hairbrush. Should I go back home? No, I need to get to the hospital. The decision overwhelms me.

Laura is still heavily sedated. I talk to her about Sylbuster, and tell her quietly how sorry I am that I didn't save her, and how I'll make it up to her.

A steady stream of friends comes to visit, even though they can't see Laura. Only relatives. I go between Laura's room and the waiting room, telling the story each time, seeing the same horrified reaction. The constant repetition is taking a toll.

Someone brings a Los Angeles Times. Laura's school picture is on the front page. I wonder how they got it. The article is well-written and correct in the details. I'm glad I talked to them. Greg Ysais. That's the name of the man who saved her. Good. Now we'll be able to thank him. I put the paper aside to save it.

David peeks around the waiting room door, unsure of what to do next. I jump up and hug him; I keep him next to me. He tells stories of what happened with Linda's sons, and their normal everyday life seems like a foreign country. Don, David and I go to Cocos for dinner. David plays with his food and gets to drink as much Dr. Pepper as he wants. The waitress finally leaves the pitcher on the table. The dinner, when it's finally served, is tasteless. What if something happens to Laura and we're not there? We eat quickly and rush back.

Don and I haven't talked at all since the attack. Don is an optical engineer and talking is difficult for him. I don't understand what he does at his work, but he's a valuable employee and highly respected. He thinks very logically and emotions are hard for him.

We've always had trouble communicating. I like small talk. Don hates it. I love answering questions like, "What's your favorite color, or day, or season, or what was the happiest day of your life?"

Don says, "I hate questions like that. They're so trivial and stupid. I do like to talk about important things, like politics and philosophy and science."

"But we never talk about those things," I argue, "and besides, the trivial things are like a window into who a person really is. You can find out a lot about a person with those questions."

We have very different ways of doing things, too. A few months ago, I wanted a shelf in the back bedroom. I didn't want to wait, so I found a board in the garage and nailed some supports in the wall and put the shelf up. It was crooked, and rocked back and forth. When Don got home, I showed him the shelf and, embarrassed, asked for his help. After he sighed, down came the shelf. The new one is still being sanded and varnished to perfection in the garage, but when and if it ever gets installed, it will be part of the house forever and able to hold hundreds of pounds. And it won't rock back and forth.

Our communication is a lot like those shelves in the back room. I say whatever comes to mind, whatever I'm thinking. Most of the time it's not perfect, rocking back and forth on the nails, but at least I try to say something.

Don keeps all his emotions inside, working on them until he feels they're perfect. When he has them all figured out and carefully constructed, then he'll say something.

No wonder we can't talk to each other.

Don and I get a Coke that evening in the hospital cafeteria. We sit across from each other in silence.

I sip my Coke. It tastes like sweet vinegar. I can't think of anything to say. I stare at the Hispanic woman cleaning the tables.

Don starts talking, the first time since the attack.

"I know this is going to sound selfish, but I feel terrible about this happening at Casper's."

"What do you mean?"

"Well, I love to hike more than anything in the world. And now I'll never be able to go hiking again."

I agree. "I'll never go hiking again."

"I don't blame you. But sometimes I think that's what keeps me going, knowing that I can go up to the Sierras for backpacking and hiking with the family and being out in the wilderness. I'm never going to be able to do that again."

I don't know what to say.

I think of Don and me hiking up to Lake Ediza in the Sierras. After two strenuous days of backpacking and adapting to the altitude, of dusty trails and sore feet, we made it to the lake, threw our backpacks on the grassy slope, and lay down in a field of flowers. White clouds dotted the sky, but I saw dark clouds on the horizon. They rolled in quickly. I heard thunder, and then a sudden downpour drenched us. The thunder, instead of being "up there," was right on top of us, rolling back and forth across the wide valley. It hurt my ears, and there was nowhere to run, so we just lay in the flowers and got completely soaked. Then, as quickly as the clouds rolled in, they swept down the valley. We could see the rain move away in sheets toward the mountain peaks. The sun came out and we put up our tent and dried out in front of a smoky fire.

Don was most himself when he was hiking. When we came home, he left part of his soul behind.

When we discovered Casper's Park close to home, he was thrilled. It was wonderful to take the kids with us and show them the beauty of beetles, live oak trees, and tadpoles. We learned the names of the native plants, and waded in the silvery streams. I'll never go there again. I'll never go hiking again.

Don and I head back to Laura's room. Don's father Harry calls to him from the waiting room as we pass by. He and his wife had been on a camping trip, and the CHP had finally located them. They've driven from San Luis Obispo, a five-hour drive.

Harry is a handsome 65, always with a ready laugh and a new story. He married again soon after Virginia, Don's mother, died of pancreatic cancer.

It seems as if Harry's heart is breaking when he looks at Laura, lying in the hospital bed. He tries not to cry, but calls her "my little rascal," and then he has to leave the room. Joanie looks once at Laura and then walks out, crying big tears. They go back to our house to pick up David from school.

Wednesday midnight, March 26

I'm sitting quietly with Linda, but I need to get some fresh air. The dry hospital air makes my throat hurt. The glass doors swing open and I step outside. From the dark parking lot I can see the San Diego freeway and the lights of Mission Viejo. I've lived in

California for ten years but it still doesn't feel like home. My parents and sisters are back in St. Louis and my heart yearns for all the seasons of the Midwest.

Still, the moist night air feels good on my skin. Suddenly I feel like someone is watching me. Fear blows over me like an icy wind as I whirl around.

Only the dark night surrounds me. I peer down the hill to the brush and manzanita, but fear washes over me. My mouth is dry as I step back towards the dim light over the back door. A few cars are parked in the lot but I don't see anyone. I feel sick, just like the attack is happening all over again.

Keeping watch, still backing up, I open the door and slip into the safety of the hospital, my heart pounding. I lean on the wall till I can breathe again. I've seen the attack day and night in my mind, but this was different. I felt like I was back in the stream, with the water swirling around my ankles.

In the waiting room I sit quietly, my head nodding till I bump the wall and wake up. I grab a pillow and cram it behind my head.

Linda shakes my arm.

"Look."

I glance up to see a school picture of Laura on the late night news.

A gruesome close-up of a dead mountain lion flashes on the screen. I jump up quickly and turn the volume higher. The picture pans out to the bed of a pick-up truck.

The man who shot the lion looks proud with his rifle. I squint at the screen, trying to see the animal. The lion is thin and emaciated. I can see its ribs. A county representative is saying, "We think that the lion might have been someone's pet and they let it go and now it's starving. That's probably why it attacked the little girl."

"It's not the right lion." I stare at the screen in disbelief.

"You don't think so? But they're saying they killed it today in the same area. It must be." Linda sounds barely awake.

"I know that's what they're saying, but the lion didn't look at all like that. It was much bigger." If that lion weighs 90 lbs., then the one that attacked Laura had to weigh at least 150 lbs. It was a huge, muscular animal, not this poor emaciated one. I have a photograph of it in my mind.

I have to tell Don. There's another lion out there, the one that attacked Laura. But the county has killed a lion, and they're satisfied. They're going to let people back in the park and tell them it's safe.

Midnight to dawn is the longest stretch of time. I squirm in the cheap vinyl chair. I try to rest my head on the wall, but it's impossible to sleep. Sometimes I sit in Laura's room. I talk to her, but mostly I'm in the way, and I run out of things to say so quickly. It's hard when there's no response. Then I wander back out to the waiting room. Linda and I talk and I sleep a little. I can't sleep at home during the day because of the constant ringing of the telephone. And now Harry and Joanie are there, cleaning and cooking and taking care of David. Linda offers her house.

"I'll give you the key. Just go in and sleep for a few hours. No one will be there or call you." Her offer is generous. I need the sleep badly.

I drive there the next afternoon instead of home. I open the door, and no one is there. But more importantly, there are no memories here, no toys of Laura's, no phone messages, nothing to remind me of the horrible truth.

Upstairs in the quiet bedroom, I finally fall asleep. I wake in the late afternoon with the last sunlight streaming in the window. I have a few seconds of delight, feeling the cool breeze, before I remember where I am and what has happened. I savor the seconds of not remembering, but they're gone so quickly, like a dream.

I hurry back to the hospital. The phone rings in the waiting room. I answer it.

"Sue, it's Mike Madigan from choir. I'm really sorry to hear about Laura. I want you to know that if there's anything I can do, I'll be glad to help."

Mike is a tenor with thinning red hair. He drives a mauve Rolls Royce, and has corrected everyone who says it's pink. The car was a gift from someone. He seems happily married, with a lovely wife and two girls a little older than Laura. No one knows exactly what he does, and he just smiles when people ask him. In our small Catholic choir, he's always a topic of conversation.

Just last week he asked about piano lessons for his two girls. It was the first time I had ever talked to him.

"I'm a private investigator, and her attack took place on county property, so if you want me to look into the county's liability, just let me know."

"Thanks, Mike. I really appreciate it. We're just hoping that Laura makes it through the week."

We talk for a few more minutes and he gives me his office number, but I can't think of why we would need Mike. Why would the county have anything to do with Laura? Who cares if they own the park?

Wednesday goes by slowly. Laura lies unmoving, still breathing through a respirator. She's getting rabies shots and a brain infection is still possible. Hundreds of people have called to help. But no one can help with what we want the most-to have our child back, whole and beautiful.

When I get home, a big manila envelope stuffed in the mailbox catches my attention. I tear it open as I walk inside, and pull out a letter.

"Dear Mr. Small,

I am extremely sorry to hear about your daughter being attacked by the mountain lion. I know that to read this letter and accompanying documents will be very painful. But I ask you to please do so, that maybe you can prevent this from happening to another child.

It was no coincidence that your daughter was attacked. The conditions that caused the attack were put into motion some years back by the Calilfornia Department of Fish and Game."

The letter says that the overhunting of deer permitted by the state of California has reduced the number of deer available to the mountain lion. Because the lions have no food, they venture closer and closer to civilization to find prey. And now the mountain lion is protected by a moratorium, so they're increasing in numbers.

The letter is signed by Tom Elsbury, president of the California Deer Hunters Association. He's included pamphlets on deer in the Santa Ana Mountains. I have no idea what he's talking about. I don't know anything about deer or mountain lions and I've never heard of a mountain lion moratorium. I show Don the letter that night.

He reads it slowly. "I have no idea what this is about. Maybe you should call your friend from choir. He did offer to help."

Wednesday, March 26

The television stations want an update on Laura, so they schedule a small press conference with Dr. Palmer, Dr. Watanabe, Don and me. We sit behind a large folding table in a conference room at the hospital. The cameras start rolling.

First they ask about Laura and Dr. Palmer answers. The second question takes me by surprise.

"What is your opinion about the mountain lion moratorium?"

"Uh, I'm only concerned about Laura's recovery."

"Are you going to sue the county of Orange?"

I answer quickly. "We're just interested in Laura right now."

Luckily the next question is for Dr. Palmer, about Laura's head injuries.

The press conference is over quickly, but I wonder about the reporter's questions. There's a lot going on that we know nothing about. I don't want to sue anyone. Why would we sue the County of Orange?

When I check on Laura, the nurse says there hasn't been any change. She hasn't awakened yet, and I sit by her bed for a few minutes.

As Don leaves he turns to me, "Call Mike. Ask him about the letter."

I dig through my purse and find Mike's number on a scrap of paper.

"Mike, it's Sue, Laura's mom. Yes, thanks. She's doing a little better. I got this letter from a man named Tom Elsbury. He's head of some deer hunter's association and he says that the attack could have been prevented. Could you read the letter and tell us what you think? Or maybe call him and talk to him? Oh, and there's one other thing. When Don went back to the park on Sunday, the ranger told him that, let's see, 'they'd been having trouble with that mountain lion recently.' That's exactly what he said."

"They knew the mountain lion was there! And they didn't tell you!"

"Nobody said anything to us, and we even asked when we went in the park if there were any problems."

"Is it ok if I come down to talk to you?"

"Sure. Don should be down here this evening after work."

A steady stream of visitors keeps me busy for the next few hours. I love all of them for coming, but I wish visiting hours were over. I finally slump down in the chair and close my eyes until Mike walks in. He shakes my hand firmly. It seems like we've known each other for a long time.

"Can I see Laura?"

"Of course." I sneak him back to her room, the uncle that she doesn't have. Mike's two girls are just a few years older than Laura. I can see the compassion on his face, and a touch of something else. Maybe anger, or perhaps the thought of his girls lying in Laura's place. Back out in the waiting room, we talk easily till Don comes, and then I do the introduction. Mike suggests we go to the small back room where no one can hear our conversation. Glass windows separate it from the main waiting room.

Mike is quite a talker. He says that the fact the county knew about the mountain lion and didn't warn us, is reason enough for a lawsuit. I'm surprised at the suddenness of this talk about a lawsuit. He's confident and persuasive, but I shake my head. I don't want to sue anyone, and neither does Don. I just want to understand what Elsbury was talking about in his letter.

Mike reads the letter. "Can I get your permission to call him?"

I can feel his excitement. He can hardly wait to find out what's going on.

"Sure," Don says.

"Did anyone give you a warning of any kind?"

"No, nothing," Don explains. "There was even a ranger at the entrance. We stopped when we paid our fee and asked if there were any problems. I was really concerned about the road being flooded, and he assured us it was fine, but he could have told us then if there were any other problems. And he didn't say a word. Just gave us the usual pamphlet and waved us on."

"What does the pamphlet say?" Mike keeps digging.

I answer that one. "It gives a description of the park, including the trails. It even says in one place that the most dangerous thing in the park is poison oak, something like that. Don and I have talked about it before. That's why I always felt it was safe."

Mike sits up straighter. "Do you have the pamphlet?"

I think for a few seconds. "I guess it's still in our car, maybe under the front seat."

Don goes to get the pamphlet. He hands it to Mike, who's talking to me about immunities or something.

"It says, 'Be careful of the most dangerous form of wildlife in the park—poison oak.' Do you mind if I keep this?"

Don shakes his head. "Go ahead and take it. We're not going to need it."

"I want to talk to a lawyer friend of mine in San Francisco. I think you have a case against the county of Orange. They own the park."

We agree to let Mike call his friend. I don't think it'll amount to anything, but I'm touched that Mike, whom I barely know, cares enough to help. He seems kind in spite of his rough exterior.

I'm angry that the ranger knew about the lion, but a lawsuit? And the pamphlet was pretty misleading, especially to a city girl like myself, who didn't know any better. But I push the anger aside. I have to concentrate on Laura.

Around midnight, I walk out the sliding glass door at the back of the hospital. I'm thinking about Laura, and forget about the terror I felt last night. But I don't forget for long.

The fear comes quickly, its intensity grabbing my chest and heart. I can't breathe. I have to get back inside. My hand is on the door. I'm ready to pull it open and rush in, but I wait. I'm safe. I'm ok. Nothing is happening, I tell myself. I breathe deeply. Just wait a few more seconds. There's nothing out here. Nothing but the empty parking lot, the hills beyond, and the night above.

Slowly I'm aware of a faint sound, a steady splashing of water, like the stream. Steady, swirling water. A dripping sound. I look around. A grey faucet next to the door is almost hidden in the dim light. The glow from the pale light makes the bushes, the wall and the faucet the same ash gray. Steady slow drips of water plop onto the mud below.

I close my eyes and I'm in the stream again. The mountain lion is rushing toward Laura and I'm powerless. I can hear the water in the stream. I open my eyes. I clench the door tightly. I watch the faucet drip. The feeling of terror gradually subsides.

My life has become a tiny box, closing in on all sides by those moments at the park. My sleep, my dreams, my house, my faith; all of them are being crushed as the box closes in on me. I pull open the door and walk back inside. It's all I can do.

Chapter 5

Thursday, March 27

I'm sitting next to Laura when a nurse taps me on the shoulder.

"There's someone in the waiting room asking for you."

I get up slowly, dreading another visitor. Another retelling of the story. Another "Yes, we're doing ok. Thanks for coming."

I really do appreciate all of our friends; I'm just not able to handle another visitor right now.

I walk into the waiting room. Greg Ysais is standing alone by the door. Tears come to my eyes.

"I was just wondering how Laura was doing?"

"A little better. Would you like to see her?"

"Yes, if I could."

I touch his hand. "I can't thank you enough for what you did. Don and I are so grateful."

Greg looks down. "Anybody would have done the same thing."

I don't say it, but in my heart I know that's not true. Only special people do what Greg did. To put your life in danger to save someone else. They're called heroes. And that's what Greg is.

We walk in Laura's room together. He stares silently at Laura for a few minutes, then turns to leave.

"I hope she gets better. Have the doctors said much?"

"No, just getting her through the next few days is really important."

I take his hand. "Thank you so much."

Greg turns and leaves.

Don is holding Laura's hand later that afternoon when suddenly he smiles.

I look at him, puzzled.

"She squeezed my hand."

We both wait for more, but that's all the response we get. It's enough, though. Maybe there is hope. I stop myself from thinking too far ahead. No one knows the extent of Laura's injuries, except that she has extensive brain damage. It's too soon to determine if she'll walk, or speak, or remember anything.

As I sit next to her, Laura moves her right arm. It's just a tiny motion, but I'm excited. Maybe she'll recover the use of that arm. I can hardly wait to tell Dr. Palmer.

Later, I see him coming out of Laura's room, his walk brisk and purposeful. I get up to meet him at the door. I'm bursting with the news of Laura squeezing Don's hand and moving her right arm.

He stands silently in front of me, looking down at the floor. His curly black hair frames his face. Finally he looks up. I'm waiting for him to be as thrilled as I am, but his face is serious.

"We don't know yet if she's going to live, so let's not be too concerned about her arm. Remember, there's still a tremendous danger of a brain infection. The wound was very dirty, and although she's receiving massive doses of antibiotics, we don't know if that will be enough. It'll be at least ten days before she's safe." He puts his hand on my shoulder, pats it awkwardly, and then walks away.

Tears well up in my eyes as I watch his white coat disappear down the hall. I want him to be honest, but not that honest.

Friday, March 28

Dr. Watanabe won't let us watch him change the bandages on Laura's head.

"You'll see her head soon enough, and hopefully by that time it'll be a little better." I have no desire to see the scars. Some of the transplanted skin is dying, so Laura will go into surgery again on Thursday. The next day, she opens her eye for the first time and seems to be awake and aware for a few minutes. I tell myself not to get excited. Just because she can open her eye doesn't mean that she can understand anything. I'm getting as cautious as Dr. Palmer.

Mike bursts in the waiting room.

"I've called my friend, Rich Staskus from San Francisco, and he's coming down tomorrow. I think we really have a case against the county. I tried to talk to the ranger, but he wouldn't speak to me. I'm sure someone in the county told him to be quiet."

I can tell Don is angry because he's even quieter than normal. I put my hand on his leg and he slips his hand over mine.

"Do you really think we have a case?" I can't help asking Mike again.

"You have a case of negligence against the county, and they should at least pay for some of Laura's medical treatments. You have no idea what she'll need in the future."

"I know, but how can they be responsible for a wild animal?" It would be nice to have them pay for Laura's medical bills, but are they really responsible, just because the lion was there? I'm not so sure.

"They're responsible for warning the public, and they didn't. You have an incredible case, and you need to talk to Rich Staskus."

Mike can only stay a minute, and after he leaves, Don looks over at me. "I don't want to sue anybody."

I know he doesn't. He wants life to be honest and fair, like he is. He would never file a lawsuit unless he had a compelling reason.

"I know, neither do I. But they knew the lion was there, and that it was dangerous."

"I can't believe they didn't say anything."

"We should see what Mike finds out. The ranger should have said something. I mean, that's why we went to Casper's, because they had rangers and the playground for the kids. And we thought it was perfectly safe. They said it was."

Don nods. "Remember when we went to Yosemite and Yellowstone? They have written warnings there. And the rangers warn you about bears and elk and all the dangers. That's why the rangers are there. To keep the public safe."

Don believes in following the rules, and doing things correctly. He's responsible, so expects others to be responsible also. It really bothers him that we asked, and the ranger just dismissed us.

Later that night, I sit by Laura's bed. The heart monitor beeps steadily. She lies still. No more squeezing of the hand, or moving her arm, or even opening her eye.

As a nurse transfers IV bags, she looks at me and says, "Do you have a strong faith?" I answer "Yes," without thinking.

She tidies up Laura's sheets and pillows, then leaves the room satisfied. I sit wondering if in all my thirty-seven years, I ever doubted the existence of God.

As I watch Laura breathe, I think again that maybe there isn't a God. The thought makes me sick. When I first moved to California, I had a roommate. One morning I woke up suddenly in the dark. My waterbed was sloshing from side to side. I thought my roommate was playing a practical joke by jumping on the bed. Then I heard her call from her room, "It's an earthquake! Get to the door!"

I jumped up and with shaking legs made it to the door. My roommate stumbled out of her room and we stood till the swaying stopped.

I remember the excitement washing over me, taking the place of the fear. We watched news reports, and worried about people closer to the epicenter. I called my parents in St. Louis.

Life settled back to normal gradually. But my feeling about the ground changed that morning, and the firmness and permanence of the earth was wiped away. I worried about the next earthquake, and whether I would be in a tall building or on a bridge.

My belief in God feels like that first earthquake. God was always the firm ground under my feet. But in an instant, with the thought that He might not exist, the ground is swaying and buckling, and I can't get it to stop.

Chapter 6

Saturday, March 29

Laura is moved out of intensive care into a private room in pediatrics. I'm not as excited as I want to be. I'm thrilled that she's better, but worried that she might still get an infection, and terrified that she'll lose her sight or never be able to speak or think clearly. I still can't quite believe the attack happened. The past week has all blurred together. I feel like I could walk in the door at home and Laura will come running up to me and throw her arms around me. But I pull myself back to reality.

She has improved. She's in pediatrics. She can breathe on her own. She opens her eyes and sometimes tracks our movement around the room. She's trying to speak, but her mouth is swollen and the nerves slashed along one whole side of her face. Dr. Palmer says it might be a long time before she can speak. There's still danger of a brain infection, but he admits that it grows less with every day. I'm worried that she won't have the constant nursing care that she had in intensive care.

As I'm bringing a large plastic bag of stuffed animals, posters, and movies to Laura's room, I hear laughing from the therapy room off the hall. David's sitting at the low play table with a scruffy young man with long hair. They're flicking a wadded-up piece of paper across the table. I don't know who the man is, but I don't want some stranger talking to David.

"You got one point, but that's it!" he yells.

"No, that's three. It made it over the line," David laughs, and picks up the wad of paper from the floor.

David sees me at the door and waves. The man stands up, pushing back his shoulder-length mop of hair.

"We were just playing some table football," he apologizes. His clothes hang on him and his loafers are scuffed and worn, like a college student. An overflowing leather briefcase is thrown on the floor.

"You must be Sue. I'm Rich Staskus, the lawyer from San Francisco." He extends his hand. I quickly adjust my thinking from, "Who the hell are you?" to "This is the lawyer who will help us." He doesn't look much like a lawyer. We talk for a few minutes and I take him to see Laura while David wanders off to the vending machines down the hall.

Don arrives and a nurse shows the three of us to an empty room where we can talk privately. Mike knocks at the door a few minutes later. Rich wants to get a video of Laura's injuries, today or tomorrow at the latest, then asks us to narrate the story into his small tape recorder.

When we finish, Rich smiles politely. I wish I had told the story better.

"Well, there might be a case here, but I'm not sure. The county has so many immunities from prosecution that it's going to be very difficult to win in court."

Mike sits up straighter. "We have what the ranger said to Don and the letter from Elsbury. I know we have a case."

Rich can't seem to get comfortable in the hard wooden chair. He finally pulls a few papers out of his briefcase and hands them to Don.

"A government has to be protected. They need to send soldiers to war and ask their citizens to risk things for the good of the country or state, and they can't be held responsible for everything. If this were a private corporation, like that Lion Country Safari case here a few years ago, you wouldn't have any problem. But going up against the government is difficult."

"They knew the lion was there. And there's the brochure!" Mike is trying too hard. This isn't a good sign. A few days ago, Mike made it sound like Rich was not only willing but excited. I don't want a lawyer who's ambivalent about our chances.

I don't want to sue anyone, but I do want to find out why the park knew about the mountain lion and didn't warn us.

Rich says, "I'm going to go back to San Francisco and work on this awhile. I'll get back to you really soon. I still want that video team to get Laura on tape. You have no idea how important this will be if we ever go to trial." Don and I sign the papers making Rich our lawyer and shake hands with him.

As Rich disappears down the hall, Mike reassures us with his irrepressible excitement.

"I know you have a case."

"But Rich said the county had too many immunities."

Mike waves the immunities away with his hand. "You can win this easily."

I don't want to win anything. I just want Laura to get better.

"Mike, we really don't want to sue anyone."

"I know. But let Rich and I do some work on this before you decide. Oh, one other thing. I gave the county a written request for the police report, but they won't release it."

Don speaks up. "The police report is public, isn't it?'

"Yeah." Mike sounds angry. "They're required to give it to us, but they're refusing. I wonder what they're hiding. Don't worry, I'll get it. It'll just take some time."

I remember the news from the other night. "Mike, there's one other thing. That lion they shot and killed isn't the right one. It was too small and emaciated."

"The lion they shot a few days ago?"

"Yeah, the one in the back of a pickup truck."

"You're sure?"

"I'm positive." That poor sick mountain lion was not the one that grabbed Laura. I know the lion is still out there. Why doesn't anyone ask me if that was the right lion? I saw it. Don't they worry about someone else getting attacked?

Saturday evening, March 29

Don stays with Laura while I go to the Easter Vigil. Linda and I started the choir seven months ago.

She's the director and I'm her accompanist, and I want to be there for our first Easter.

I arrive as the choir is walking into church after rehearsal. Everyone wants to know about Laura. I thank them and tell the story briefly to a crowd of people. It's a relief to walk inside the church for the long service instead of talking. For the next few hours I really believe that Christ has risen from the dead. Maybe I missed this basic concept of Christianity, that we must experience the death before we have the resurrection to a new life. Maybe Laura's attack is the beginning of her resurrection. How close I feel to understanding. And then, as I leave the church, the feeling slips away in the cool night air.

The parking lot slowly empties until only a few cars are left and a small knot of people stand under the light at the church entrance. I sit inside the car, my head back and eyes closed. The frightening thought comes back with a vengeance. What if we're in this all alone and there is no God? I want to bask in the beauty of the Easter Vigil, but the idea is relentless.

I drive home to a silent house, and slip into bed quietly, but my thoughts roller coaster up and down all night. I'm thankful to God for saving Laura's life, but why did he let it happen in the first place? When I think of the great doctors, our wonderful friends, and all the help we're receiving, I'm thrilled. But when I think of Casper's Park, the ranger who said nothing, the silence of God, and the extent of her injuries, I'm sick.

The lion seems like a force of evil, engulfing my life and thoughts, but I know it wasn't really evil. It was only being a lion. But there were people who knew the lion was there and didn't warn us. That was the real evil. But why is there evil in the world at all?

I turn over again and plump up the pillow. Of course there are explanations for evil. I've heard them all my life. I have a degree in theology. God gives us free will, and some people choose evil. We couldn't choose the good if there wasn't the bad. That explanation was drilled into my head for over thirty years, but now that I see Laura's suffering, the words seem empty.

They don't explain earthquakes or natural disasters that kill hundreds of thousands of people. Those are acts of God, and He must have a reason for them. But what's the reason? He could have created the earth so that there would be no earthquakes or tornadoes, but He hadn't. And it doesn't explain illness and death. When I think about it, I can't really find a good explanation for so much suffering and pain. All the answers used to make sense. Now I'm not so sure.

I am afraid, though, of offending this God who might be in control of all our lives. Maybe he's not as loving and caring as I hoped. He permitted this mountain lion attack. Why did he let it happen? Everything I thought about God, his goodness and kindness and love, seems a cruel joke.

How could I ever think that He was kind and good? He lets horrible things happen to people all the time. I can't seem to get rid of the bleak, horribly depressing void that has opened up in front of me. I turn over again and watch the dim light dawn outside the window. Sleep is impossible.

Monday, March 31

When I arrive home late in the afternoon, David peeks out of his door and says hi.

"Come here, honey." I give him a quick hug. I grab two cans of Dr. Pepper from the refrigerator and discover a chocolate cake someone made for dessert. I can see Harry and Joanie out in the backyard, drinks in hand, sitting in the lounge chairs. I clear off David's backpack from the table and we sit down with the drinks and two slices of cake.

I have no idea what happened to David on the day of the attack. "What happened after you came running back with Dad?"

"Dad told me to get help, so I ran across the stream and tried to find someone. Then the man who saved her, Greg, came running towards me and I stopped him and told him that we needed help and which way to go. Then I kept running back down the trail to get more help."

"Wow, I had no idea you were such a big help. You really helped save your sister."

David tries to look like he doesn't care, but I reach over and give him a hug. "I'm so proud of you."

"I think I helped save her."

"I know you did."

I see his shy smile, the same smile of delight in dinosaurs and airplanes, a smile still full of childhood wonder. I wish we could talk more, but Harry and

Joanie came inside from the backyard. I don't know what else to do for David right now. He's going to have to be on his own for a while.

My parents call every day, wanting to fly out. I love them both and my mom will be a big help, but I hesitate. I'm not really sure why. I walk outside to the neglected back yard and sit on a white plastic chair by the peach and apricot trees. It's going to take months to get back to normal.

I look around the yard. In my mind, I can see David roller-skating on the patio, David and Laura giggling as they slide down a sheet of wet plastic on the back slope. I remember spraying the hose on them as they screamed with laughter. I look over at the vegetable garden, and remember picking tomatoes, trying to teach Laura not to pick all the green ones. The playhouse I built for a woodworking class stands empty by the fence. There will be no more normal.

I don't want mom and dad to see how bad things are. I want to show them what a good marriage I have, what perfect children, and my very successful career teaching piano. Now all that lies shattered on the ground, and I don't know how long it will take to glue all those pieces back together, if I ever can. But I can't wait any longer for their much-needed help. I walk inside and call them.

They call back in a few minutes with plane reservations.

Chapter 7

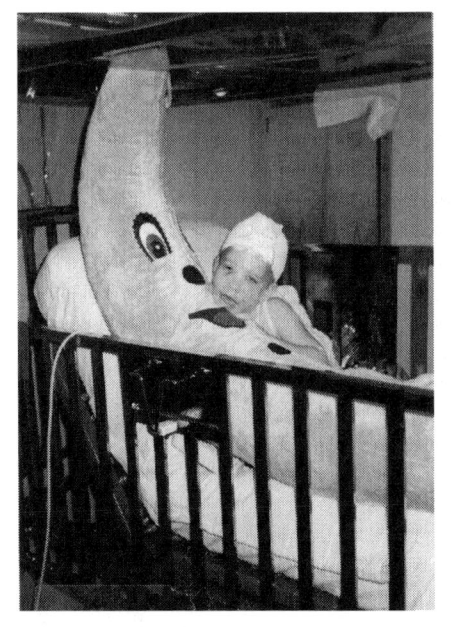

Laura and banana

April 3

Harry, Don's father, and his wife Joanie, leave after a few days, but luckily my parents will give us some much needed help. Mike picks my parents up from Los Angeles in his Rolls Royce. It was sweet of him to offer. He likes impressing people. I wait in Laura's hospital room till they arrive. I'm still worried about my mom and dad. They're in their seventies, and I feel they should be insulated from this pain. If they aren't strong enough, I know I can't help them. Laura sits propped up in her bed when mom and dad arrive. Mom smiles bravely through her tears and hugs Laura. My dad stands there not knowing quite what to do. I ask them how their plane ride was, and Mom jokes, "It was fine, except for a few potholes."

Laura laughs. She's really laughing. Could she have understood the joke? She's heard my mom talk about the potholes in St. Louis after the winter snow. I feel a glimmer of hope.

Laura moves her left hand back and forth on the blankets like she's writing something. I hand her a pencil and put a piece of paper on a clipboard in front of her. She starts to draw with her left hand, even though she was right-handed. A box appears, then a simple but unmistakable bow on the top.

"Is that a present for grandma and grandpa?"

Laura nods her head and keeps writing. Her right hand lies motionless on the blanket but her left hand is writing letters, the ones she just learned in pre-school. She prints "LAURA," and hands it to me. I start to cry. In that one beautiful second I realize that Laura's mind is functioning-she knows who she is, who we are, how to write her name, and she has her memory. Most important of all, she's still LAURA. She can still laugh. She still wants to give others gifts. I know she has incredible struggles ahead, but for that one moment, our Laura is back.

My mom is crying, too. Laura looks confused. She has no idea why we're crying. I give her a hug and tell her how wonderful she is.

In my excitement, I notice my dad off to the side of the bed. He doesn't seem to realize what just happened. I'm thrilled about Laura, but in the back of my mind I wonder what's happening to my dad.

April 4

The next morning, Dad comes back in the house after a short walk. I hear him ask Mom in his heavy German accent, "Why are we out here in California?"

"Because of Laura. You know that."

"What? What happened to Laura?" He's really upset. Mom calms him and tells him again that Laura has been attacked and is in the hospital. He has no recollection of it.

I slip back in the bedroom and sit down on the unmade bed. Mom doesn't know I heard them. She told me Dad was having a few memory problems but I never imagined it was this bad. I can't think about this now. There are just too many things to cry about. I'll think about it another time. I stand up, wipe my eyes, walk out into the kitchen, and wish them a good morning. Mom makes a quick breakfast for me, and I head down to the hospital.

The tubes are removed from Laura's nose and mouth this morning, and we wait anxiously for her to talk. But five more days go by, and she still can't make a meaningful sound. She tries, but no one can understand her. How frustrating for Laura. She's only five, and has gone through this horrible trauma, and now, she can't even say a word. My heart aches for her.

When she can eat solid foods, she'll be able to get off the IV. Every day the nurse asks her what she wants for lunch, encouraging her to try some food. One morning Laura makes a circle with her thumb and finger.

The nurse asks, "You want macaroni?"

Laura shakes her head.

"Cheerios?"

No.

"Lifesavers?"

Laura looks more frustrated.

"Donuts?"

Laura nods her head. That's it. The kitchen sends up two donuts immediately. By the end of the day, Laura has us all trained. Make the circle and we'll get her a donut. She has her day of donuts, and then we have to start saying no. But at least she gets off the I.V.

Now I'm certain that the "old" Laura is inside, waiting to come back. That hope of getting my Laura back keeps me going. Whatever physical injuries she has, whether it includes blindness, paralysis, seizures, or learning disabilities, pales in importance to the fact that she is alive. That Laura, full of curiosity and humor and intelligence, is there beneath the surface, under the scars.

April 5

We won't know the extent of Laura's head injuries for a long time. Writing her name and responding to our questions is tremendously encouraging. Each day I hear another word I almost understand.

When her breakfast tray arrives, she gets a milkshake, Jello, bananas for potassium, plus the occasional donut. She gets a banana at each meal, but can't possibly eat three bananas a day. We even start joking about them. I pick up the spoon to help her with her cereal but she grabs it. She is determined, as usual, to do everything herself. I would always get so annoyed because she wouldn't accept any help. Now I realize how important her independent spirit will be.

As I step outside her room, I look down the long corridor and see a woman carrying what looks like a huge stuffed banana. God, I hope the banana isn't for Laura. It would take up half the room! And Laura already has a million stuffed animals. I try to duck back inside her room, but the woman walks right up to me.

"Are you Laura's mom? I thought I recognized you. I'm the ambulance driver, and I just wanted to see how she's doing."

She holds out the banana. "And I thought Laura might like this."

I try not to laugh as she deposits the banana into my arms like a huge baby.

"Thank you so much. Laura is doing better."

Laura smiles widely at the six-foot yellow stuffed banana.

"There was an elephant there too, but I decided to get the banana." I thank her again, wondering why she would get either one.

When the lady leaves, we both laugh. The banana is much larger than Laura, with a green felt mouth and black eyes with felt eyelashes. The yellow material is soft and fuzzy. I prop all six feet of it up in the corner of the room, like a fuzzy yellow exclamation point. What we'll ever do with it, I can't imagine.

At least five doctors stop by every morning and evening. Nurses wander in and out all day, and family and good friends. I ask a child psychologist to talk to Laura. As she comes to the door, Laura turns her head away and yells very clearly, "Get out."

Hearing her speak so clearly for the first time, I almost overlook her rudeness. The psychologist asks Laura if she can come back at a different time. Laura nods her head. I'm thrilled that she finally said a word clearly. It gives me such hope. And even though it was rude, and unfortunately directed at the psychologist, I really do understand why she yelled. I feel the same way about the number of people who are coming to visit, hour after hour, day after day, without a break. My smile is pasted on.

I'm almost back to Laura's door with a drink when I hear someone else in her room. I see an elderly volunteer sitting in the chair next to her bed.

"Oh, that mountain lion didn't want to hurt you. She was just going to take you to see her babies."

I walk quickly in the door, furious at what I just heard.

"Get out, just get out."

The volunteer has gray hair and looks up at me in confusion. Her eyes fill with tears. But Laura doesn't need to hear lies. She's gone through a horrible experience and doesn't need to hear baby stories. I walk to the bed, shaking with anger. The woman slips out the door behind me.

"Laura, I don't like what that lady said. I hope you know it isn't true. That mountain lion meant to kill you, and we're all really happy that he didn't. It doesn't mean he was bad or horrible. He was just doing what mountain lions do. They get their food by killing other animals."

Laura needs to know the truth. What else could we possibly tell her but the truth? "Taking her to see her babies!" I'm so angry. I walk out to the nurse's station and ask for a big piece of paper.

"All visitors, please check with the nurse's station first." I tape it to her door.

April 9

Now that Laura's in pediatrics, I can stay in her room at night. She sleeps fitfully, coughing often. The meager night-light keeps the room in shadows, and I can barely make out the hastily drawn pictures from her classmates. The banana stands at attention in the corner, its mouth in a frozen smile.

I look out the small window to the concrete parking lot. The view is dry and lifeless. Laura's breathing becomes more regular, and footsteps come and go in the hallway. The sound of doctors being paged whispers through the closed door, and water is running in the next room.

I toss and turn on the small cot, reliving the incident with the volunteer. I force myself to think about something else.

As I stare through the dark window to the light in the parking lot, I remember the windows in the convent. Without my two windows, one at the head of my bed and the other at my side, I might have left the convent that first year.

The single frosted light bulb on our dormitory ceiling was turned off at exactly nine o'clock every night by the Mother Superior, and the rule of silence was enforced from then till after breakfast. Instead of sleeping, I'd lie on my stomach and look out my window. One window looked down to Kitchen Square and across to the ghostly gray chapel. I could see the dark stained glass of the chapel windows. By the time the sun rose, I would be in the chapel, watching the gray glass change to rich reds and blues.

The other window looked down at the dark road below and the green lawns stretching far in the distance. I could see lights in the small brick homes, and wondered about the people who lived in them.

I slept with both windows open wide that first summer. I had to unlock the painted white latches and push hard on the brittle chipped wood to get them to go up. I propped open the window with a wooden ruler. Crickets and cicadas were deafening in the sultry night. My prayers, thanking God for all of creation, were so much more real than the recited prayers in chapel.

Some nights I'd wake to the sound of thunder and welcome the drops of rain hitting the windows, cooling the air for a few hours. The lightning would illuminate the whole sky like a sequence of camera flashes. Each flash turned the square into a sudden gray picture, its image frozen in my mind like an old black and white photograph before it faded away in the darkness.

An electric light high on the motherhouse lit up the square and cast its shadows across the buildings. I could see the rain in huge sheets, pushed by the storm winds, blowing across the square. Wave after wave of blowing rain beat against the brick buildings.

When winter came I would wipe off the frost to see the flurries of snow in the light. I loved to watch it for hours into the night, its quiet softness silently but steadily spinning a web of white over the concrete square and the roof far above.

The twinkling lights of the homes would be lost in the swirling snow. The frosts delicate lines spun across the windows like a web. After a while, I'd lie down to sleep with the warm blankets wrapped tightly around me.

Sometimes the wind would come in through the crack of my window, and I'd wake up freezing, but gradually winter turned into spring and soon the wind brought the softness of warm spring rain. Those were the best nights, when the sound of rain lulled me to sleep, when all creation was green, and the warm soft wind would blow the raindrops under the eaves and through the screen to my windowsill.

No matter how many long lectures or endless hours of prayer there were during the day, I knew I could escape at night to my windows. Our small cubicles held a bed and a dresser. The bed had a thin mattress and a plain white bedspread. There were no pictures on the walls. Nothing sat on top of my dresser, no pictures of family or friends, nothing from my previous life.

There were two other classmates in the room, but I don't even remember their names. We never talked. The white bed curtains were always drawn. I don't remember them at all.

My friends were the wind, the rain, and the stars in the night sky.

A nurse comes quietly in Laura's room, bringing me back to the present. What happened to the beauty of God's creation? Will I ever be able to enjoy it again, or will I always be terrified of it? And the certainty that it was His creation, his glorious gift to us, seems to be gone. The nurse leaves and I sit up on the cot, looking at the sterile parking lot. All I can see is a pool of white from the tall security light lighting up a concrete barrier and one small weed. How ugly it has all become.

Chapter 8

April 10

My friend Rhonda, a parent of one of Dave's classmates, has set up a trust fund for Laura. She told me that with all the publicity, we should provide a way people could help.

"You don't need any more stuffed animals, do you?" were her words, and I numbly agreed. Rhonda did all the work. Today the bank called, so late in the afternoon I stop by.

The bank manager shakes my hand, asks how Laura is doing, and hands me three bulging mail sacks with US Postmaster printed on the burlap material. They're filled with letters to Laura. Two tellers help me drag them to the car.

Mom and I dump part of one bag out on the dining room table that evening. The original article from the *LA Times* was sent out all over the country, and there are thousands of letters. Mom is thrilled to help me go through them. I know that she wants to help, so this is perfect for her to do. Most of the letters include checks or a small amount of cash. I deposit money in the bank every few days for some unknown future. I can't believe the kindness of so many strangers.

Many of the letters addressed to Laura are from children. Most are pictures, and I put some of them up in her hospital room.

Every evening I come home from the hospital to find a dinner in the refrigerator. Volunteers from church and school bring them to the house every afternoon. I'm amazed at the number of people who are helping us.

The mountain lion attack on a five-year old has attracted national attention. I look at the overflowing letters on the dining room table with awe and appreciation. But I feel bad for the unknown victims of traffic accidents or illnesses, ones who don't have the exciting story to tell. I hope they have people who care about them.

April 11

One evening after dinner I walk in the living room. My piano is freshly dusted, but it's been weeks since I've touched it. I canceled all thirty-five of my piano students and don't know what will happen to my teaching career. I sit down, then start to play a Partita by Bach, my favorite composer. My fingers are stiff and the music hangs in the air, ugly and meaningless. It has lost its power to move me. Music seems so trivial compared to what has happened to Laura. I don't even turn the first page, but get up and walk outside.

Mom asks me to play a few days later and I play my old standby since 4th grade, *Malaguena*. It sounds good and I know Mom and Dad enjoy listening, but I feel nothing except a vague relief when I hit the final chord.

When I was five years old I started taking lessons from a gray-haired lady named Mrs. Sale. A few weeks later, I had to play an F# in a piece. I didn't understand how to do it and cried till mom let me quit. I don't remember the teacher's reaction, just the tears. But I couldn't stay away from the piano, and I started lessons again a year later.

I loved classical music. We had an old record player, a big tan piece of wooden furniture by the front window. I listened to *The Nutcracker* over and over again, carefully lifting the diamond needle back to the beginning of the black record. I knew every note and could listen to it in my head whenever I wanted. When I got older, I loved Bach, the way the music curled around itself endlessly. No one ever told me to love music; it found its way into my heart all by itself.

I accompanied every choir from grade school through college. I majored in music and taught it in high school, got a masters degree in music, and taught piano full time. But now my piano is a dead piece of furniture, just taking up room.

April 12

As I walk into Laura's room the next morning, the nurse is carrying her to the bathroom.

I hear her say, "Laura, have you seen yourself in the mirror?'

"No."

I try to get to the bathroom as the nurse holds her up to the mirror. But I'm too late.

The nurse says breezily, "Oh, I think it's a good idea for her to see herself and then she can see the improvement later on."

I'm seething inside but don't want to yell. The damage is done and there's nothing that can take it away. Laura doesn't react. She seems tired as she turns her head and closes her eyes. I don't say anything, but I'm tired of people taking control of our lives and doing what they think is best. I hope it wasn't as hard for Laura to see herself as it was for me the first time.

I want to talk to her, to tell her that she will be beautiful again, that she is always beautiful to me, but the words just can't come out.

April 15

The morning light filters through the open blinds. Laura is still asleep, the yellow banana at her side. Her right arm lies still and cool outside the blanket. She can move it, but her thumb is tucked into her hand and the other fingers curled into a permanent fist. I glance at the wall across from her bed. A large crayon poster covers it, filled with drawings and pictures from her preschool friends. Balloons droop sadly along the floor.

Laura wakes up slowly and says hi. Her smile is crooked. Her mouth only goes up on the left side. After breakfast she wants to watch cartoons, so I close the blinds. Grey clouds line the sky, and the asphalt is wet with a cold mist unusual for April.

Miss Roberta, her preschool teacher, knocks gently at the door. Miss Roberta has stopped by every single day for the last month, bringing books, tapes, crayons, anything that's perfect for a five-year old. Today she has a plastic egg full of silly putty. Maybe Laura will be able to squeeze it with her right hand. Miss Roberta tells me that Laura's classmates are scared and worried. They don't understand what happened and are afraid they will get attacked too. Roberta tells them how Laura is improving. She's been fitted for a brace and is walking, holding onto the rails in the corridor. A month ago, I would get so annoyed at Laura for always wanting to do everything herself. That determination is her best ally now.

Mike usually parks his Rolls Royce right outside her window. He comes to see her almost every day, and I look forward to seeing him. If he doesn't show up at the hospital, he's sure to call with a new joke or story about the investigation. He's thrown himself into this with an energy that amazes me. I can talk to him more easily than I can talk to Don.

One afternoon I see Mike's mauve Rolls Royce pull up outside Laura's window. A few minutes later, he knocks at the door, pulls up a chair, and tells me about the previous day.

"You know I called Mike Elsbery, the head of the Deer Hunter's Association?"

"Yeah."

"Well, I didn't want to talk on the phone. I needed to record his statement, so I met him out past Ortega Highway at his place. I brought a six-pack of beer, and we had a nice long talk. Interesting guy. He explained the mountain lion moratorium."

"I sure don't understand it."

"I'll try to explain what he said." Mike pulls out some notes.

I listen carefully, but it's difficult to understand a political issue many years after it started. The moratorium has been in place for over fourteen years. The environmentalists want the mountain lion declared an endangered species and never hunted again, but the Department of Fish and Game thinks that the mountain lion population is increasing too rapidly in urban areas, like Orange County. The NRA supports hunting, and the deer hunters realize the mountain lions are killing off all the deer, so they're for the hunting of the mountain lion.

Mike says some people were very concerned about mountain lions interacting with humans and were worried about an attack. Some people, I'm not sure who, had warned the Department of Fish and Game and even the governor that there would be an attack if nothing was done.

Laura's attack has become a forum for everyone's opinion. There's a steady stream of letters to the editor in the *Los Angeles Times* and the *Orange County Register*, as well as commentaries on the evening news. Don and I seem to be the only ones without anything to say.

I don't know what to think. I want Laura to get better, and I refuse to comment on something I know nothing about. I've always had so many opinions over the years on politics, education, religion, and no one has ever cared. Now people from TV stations and journalists are asking what Don and I think about the mountain lion moratorium, and I don't know what to say.

I'm puzzled by the county's reaction. They won't speak to us. They won't even show us the police report. It's supposed to be a public document and Mike can't get it. Despite my wish not to cast blame, I've begun to think they're hiding something.

Maybe Mike is right. Maybe we do have grounds for a lawsuit. We still have time before we have to file it, so we don't have to decide anything yet.

April 16

I'm able to go home some nights, and I try not to worry about Laura too much. I go to bed exhausted from the reporters, the doctors, and the attempts to hold everything together in our lives. I dream about the convent, my usual frantic dream of not being able to leave, running down the corridors trying to find a way out. In the dream I hear the phone ringing. The insistent sound startles me awake. I reach for the phone on the nightstand. My heart is beating fast. It's 5:30 in the morning. Something's happened to Laura!

"Yes?"

A woman's voice whispers, "Are you the mother of the little girl attacked by the mountain lion? I can't tell you my name, because it would cost me my job, but I have some information that would help your case, I hope."

I'm wide awake.

"The Harbor, Beaches and Parks Department had a commission meeting— they have them at night. It was-I don't remember the exact date, but it was a month or two before the attack. But at that meeting they had a discussion about deer hunting. There was a warning given that if there were more deer killed, the mountain lions would turn to humans to hunt. They did go ahead and vote to continue the deer hunting. If you tell your lawyer or investigator to go to Dept. 98 of the Environmental Management Agency as soon as possible, and ask for the minutes from the meetings from the first part of this year, I'll make sure they're not destroyed."

She pauses and whispers, "It's just not right what happened to your daughter."

"Thank you."

I hear the dial tone. I fumble for a pen on the nightstand, look for a scrap of paper, and end up writing the numbers on my hand. Early morning calls with whispers about hidden information. This is crazy.

Don's already left for work, so I wait till Mike is probably up and call him.

"Sue? Is this THE Sue Mattern?" Mike always has this little silly ritual that he goes through, but I don't have time for it today.

"Yeah, listen. I got this call from a lady who wouldn't tell me who she was, but she told me if you called this number you could get some information we could use in the lawsuit."

"What kind of information?" Mike's not joking now.

"She said to call the Environmental Management Agency and ask for the minutes of this commission meeting from Harbor, Beaches and Parks, on, she couldn't remember the exact date, but said it was a few months before Laura was attacked. She wouldn't give me her name but she said it might help us with our case."

"I'll give them a call as soon as they open and I'll call you back."

Mike calls as I'm walking out the door. I run back inside.

"No one would give me the records over the phone, but I talked to a woman and she said she'd have them for me if I came to the city office. She's probably the woman who called. I'm heading there right now."

I leave the hospital early and stop at the photo store to get the pictures from Casper's Park. Later that evening, when everyone is asleep, I slip into the back bedroom and sit at our big wooden desk. I pull out the pictures from the thin paper envelope. This is the roll from the day of the attack. The camera sat blindly on the sand while our lives changed.

Laura is posing in the first picture, hands outstretched, while David bends over, watching the water intently. Then a silly picture of a cactus with Mickey Mouse ears. David sitting on a tree limb dangling his feet a few inches off the ground. A picture of Laura the Friday before the attack, dressed in the purple jumper she hates, with a wreath of fresh flowers on her head. I had forgotten about the pre-school Easter parade. At the last minute, we'd grabbed a bunch of flowers from the back yard. I sit with the pictures in my hand, and let myself cry.

I want life to be the way it was before. When Laura was in intensive care, all I could think about was the present. The hospital, Laura lying still and bandaged on that bed, the steady stream of visitors, the endless telling of the story, juggling daily life and this new life of doctors and operations. Now that we've come through the darkest days, I'm beginning to think about the past. The way life was a week ago, and how it will never be the same.

Home seems the same. Sylbuster wanders into the room. The furniture, the piano, the lemon tree in the garden, the flowers in the back yard; they haven't changed. Laura's room looks the same. Her white poster bed, toys and books, Care Bears and Strawberry Shortcake. A middle class house in affluent Orange County.

But now I try to imagine Laura back in our house. And I can't put the two pictures together in my mind. She can't speak or twirl around in her dresses, or jump. She can't run into Don's arms as he grabs her and lifts her high in the air, screaming in delight.

I cry quietly so I won't wake up my parents, then stuff the pictures in the desk drawer, and go to bed.

Chapter 9

April 23

I'm helping Laura eat her applesauce when I hear a knock at the hospital door. Three paramedics from the San Juan fire station are standing outside. One of them had gone with Laura in the helicopter. They give Laura a stuffed animal and a beautiful card that says, "To Laura, brave and courageous, who has won our hearts and our admiration."

She smiles at the stuffed animal and says thank you, shyly. They talk to her a few minutes more and as we walk out in the hall, one of them turns to me. "We were all so impressed with your daughter. She kept asking about you in the helicopter. She was so worried that you had been hurt by the mountain lion."

"Really? I didn't even know she was conscious."

"Well, she kept slipping in and out of consciousness, but she was very concerned about you. We tried to tell her that you were fine and not to worry. She asked about your husband and her brother, too. She's a remarkably brave little girl."

They all shake my hand and walk down the hall. I stand, watching them, oblivious to anything around me. I feel tears running down my face, and I don't even try to wipe them away. I'm so shocked that she was conscious. I had no idea that she had asked about us. She was worried about us. At that moment when she had lost so much blood and was close to death, and in horrible pain, she asked about us. She was thinking about me, and Don and David.

I dry my tears and walk back into Laura's room. She's fallen asleep, and I sit watching her.

What a remarkable child. I love her more than I could ever imagine, but Laura was never the perfect child. She's always been difficult. She cried incessantly from the day she was born. After months it was diagnosed as a milk allergy, and the problem went away literally overnight. But then the terrible twos started early with Laura, and never seemed to go away. She developed a real mean streak. I couldn't reason with her. She wanted her way all the time. The little girl down the street would come over and Laura would take all her toys and then hit her when she thought no one was looking. I despaired of what to do. I read lots of books about the "difficult child." I bought her a "Care Bear" book once, handed it to her, and the first thing she did was hit David on the head— hard.

In school she was an angel. At the first meeting with her pre-school teacher, I finally asked if the child we were talking about was named "Laura" and I wasn't joking. With all the glowing things that had been said, I really believed the teacher had mistaken her for someone else.

Dave was the patient one, and bore the brunt of his sister's moods. At his ninth birthday party in December, Laura had thrown a huge temper tantrum.

She wanted presents too, and we finally had to take her screaming and kicking from the room. Her crying for the next few hours, with Don as mediator, ruined the entire party for everyone. I didn't know what to do with her.

Everything with Laura was a battle, from what to wear in the morning to ice cream choices. Fighting with her was a losing proposition.

The remarks from the paramedics shine a whole new light on her. She's been talking for a week, slowly and painfully, and she has rarely complained and seems to be very grateful for all the love and help we've given her. It's like we've been given a new Laura. I hate to think it, much less say it, but maybe this new Laura will be better for us all.

April 25, 1986

Long, angry speeches fill my head as I sweep the patio. Casper's Park reopened yesterday, just one month after Laura's attack. The county said the mountain lion had been killed and that everything is now safe. They won't admit that there was a problem and they don't even consider that they might have killed the wrong lion. I've tried to tell the county what I know about the lion, but no one will take my calls.

Damn them. Damn the people at the park who knew about the mountain lion and didn't even warn us. They knew the lion was there: they knew it was stalking people, especially children. They were tracking it. But they didn't even warn us.

Just one sentence besides "have a nice day," would have been enough for me to turn back. But they didn't even do that. I hate them for this month of Laura's suffering. And for the suffering she'll have to endure for the rest of her life. At first I was angry with God, but now I can see it wasn't an act of God. It was an act of man.

I can't believe the county would reopen the park and not warn people. It gives me chills to think of some other family having their child attacked. The county doesn't care. All they're interested in is protecting themselves. If they warn visitors now, that means they should have warned us, and they'll never admit that.

I'm mad at God too. I don't care if it's wrong. If He exists, then I hate Him for what he's done to Laura. Not believing in Him would be so much easier. Then it was a random attack and had no meaning. But if God really exists, what was his role in this? And the more I try to find an answer, the more oppressive the silence becomes.

The phone rings. I run inside and grab it.

"Sue, I have the minutes from that meeting, you know, the one that lady called about."

"Is there anything in them?"

"Oh, yeah. I know why the county was going to destroy them. It's really going to help us. I got the notes from the commission meeting, and they had a meeting back in '82, before the park was made, about the construction of the trails; you know, deciding where to put them in the park. Someone who was knowledgeable about mountain lions was actually consulted, and he objected to the placement of one of the trails. The reason he gave was, listen to this, it's a quote, 'The trail goes by sensitive mountain lion denning areas.' His objection was noted in the minutes of the meeting, but the trail was made anyway." Mike paused. "It was the Bell Canyon trail, the trail you were on when Laura was attacked."

He waits a second for that to sink in. I don't say anything. Mike wants to call Rich, so I say goodbye quickly and hang up. I was angry before, but now I feel sick and shaky.

That afternoon at the hospital, I stare out the window and start thinking about the park. When I first met Don, he tried to get me to love hiking and backpacking. I didn't like doing anything dangerous and most of backpacking and hiking seemed scary to me. My mom was always worried about us breaking a leg or falling off a cliff.

Don and I would laugh privately, because Mom was so worried about everything. I didn't want to be like that. Casper's Park was perfect because they said the most dangerous thing in it was poison oak, and I took my children there with confidence.

Don comes in the room just as Dr. Watanabe arrives.

"I'm going to change the bandages on Laura's head. Would you like to stay here while I do it?" We both say yes. He's always asked us to stay out of the room, saying we weren't ready to see her head.

A month has gone by, but her shaved scalp is crisscrossed with hundreds of ugly red swollen scars.

Dr. Watanabe had told us there were over a thousand stitches. I can believe it now. I know she's lucky to be alive. But as I look at her head, I just feel like throwing up.

I bite my lip and stare at one section about two inches square, where there is no skull at all. I can see the skin pulsate with every heartbeat.

I start to whisper to Don that I have to leave the room.

But before I do, Don steps up and asks Dr. Watanabe if he can learn how to change the bandages. I stand back and watch, backing up as far as I can.

Don may not say much, but he's always there when we need him.

April 28

Laura's asleep. I'm looking out the window of her room to the darkened parking lot. I should go home. But I sit quietly for a few minutes thinking about God again. I'm still searching for that experience of God that I always thought I had, but now can't seem to find. Oh, I believed in Him strongly, His power and His benevolence. I'd pray, but I don't ever remember that I got an answer. I had more of an intellectual belief in God, not an emotional one that was complicated by prayer requests and the inevitable disappointments.

I think back to why I ever became a nun. It probably goes back to the young nun who was my speech teacher in freshman year. After she heard me play the piano, we started talking and became best friends. We discussed literature and philosophy. She was brilliant, she liked me, and she was everything I wanted to be. That was when I started thinking that the convent might not be such a bad place.

I had been the black sheep of our Catholic grade school. Most of the boys and girls went through a phase of wanting to be a priest or nun. But I always hated the thought of a vocation, and I knew I would never be a starchy, ugly nun. But my teacher friend was educated, independent and a liberal, like me, and I realized I might fit in after all. After all, the Second Vatican Council had reformed the church, and we were riding the wave of liberalism and optimism about the future. I considered the Peace Corps, but because of my friend, I chose the convent.

I believed in God, and I wanted to discover what He was really like. And I wanted to help people and change the world.

I was certain that the convent was a great place for an extrovert like me, and I was looking forward to meeting some amazing people. But at our first instruction period, I found out that I couldn't talk to most of them. The only people I could speak to were the thirty-two members of my own class. The other five hundred were off limits.

So I broke the rules. I was careful and sneaky. It was fun being defiant. I scouted out older students in other classes, who didn't care about the rules, and had some great friendships.

I was a nun for six years. I got my degree and started teaching. Theology was my minor in college, but learning what other people thought about God didn't make me any closer to Him than before.

When, after six years, I decided to leave the convent, it was easier than I thought. I hadn't taken my final vows. No one tried to talk me out of it. There were so many young sisters leaving the order, they didn't seem to care. I was glad I left when I did. The wave of liberalism and progress of the Second Vatican Council came crashing ashore and disappeared with the new conservative Pope. The reforms that were so promising were just like a wave, sinking down under the sand without a trace.

It took me all six years to realize that the Catholic Church wasn't really interested in reform, or ecumenism, or women's rights, or a more important role for the lay person. And nuns were the second-class volunteers who did the janitorial work while the priests and the hierarchy still held all the power. I didn't want to waste my life fighting a losing battle.

In all those years, although I believed strongly in God, and dedicated my life to Him, I never experienced Him once. So it's not really a surprise that He's so absent now.

Chapter 10

Home from the hospital

April 29

Almost forty days since that horrible Sunday, the doctors are ready to discharge Laura from the hospital. I'm so frightened. She can barely walk, and just taking her to the bathroom involves carrying her, undressing her, and carrying her back. She's completely helpless, and I have the added worry about her head. Every edge of furniture is a danger. I'm afraid she'll fall out of bed at night, or roll over and hit the wall with her unprotected head.

Laura is coming home tomorrow, whether I'm afraid or not. Sleep is impossible, so I get up quietly and make a cup of hot tea. My hands fold over the warm cup as I look around the family room. The edges of the furniture taunt me in the dim light. The glass-topped coffee table will come crashing down if she grabs it. It'll have to go. I've been waiting for her to come home so badly, but now I'm terrified that she'll fall down and hurt her head again. We bought her a bicycle helmet a few days ago, which she'll have to wear to protect her head. But I don't know if I can handle this homecoming. There's so much that could go wrong.

I love Laura so much. I love David too. He has the most optimism of anyone in the family and has kept me going at times when no one else could. I know it's a nine-year old boy's optimism that's based on inexperience, but everything's turned out the way he said it would. I have to try to sleep.

Morning comes quickly and Don and I rush to the hospital. Laura is sitting in her wheelchair, holding her pink bunny and yellow blanket. A photographer from the *Orange County Register* takes her picture as she's wheeled out the door of Mission Hospital. When a reporter asks what she is most excited about, she replies without hesitation, "Petting my cat, Sylbuster."

David's third grade classmates have made a huge "Welcome home, Laura" banner that covers the garage door. Don's father and stepmother are here from San Luis Obispo, and my parents are still here for a few more days. They must be anxious to get home. It can't have been easy being here this past month, cleaning and cooking and trying to help, while Don and I tried to get through one day at a time. I know Dad's memory problems aren't helping, either.

A gift of dinner is in the refrigerator, and with a few additional leftovers we sit down to eat. We're a family again. Laura is propped up in her wheelchair, her head bandaged; Mom and Dad help her hold the cup and get the food on the spoon; David talks happily in the attention of all the grandparents; Harry entertains us with his excellent stories; my dad laughs, slightly confused; Joanie talks about her latest shopping trip.

I sit back and watch. Families are messy but wonderful. Families are there when you need them. I feel like hugging everyone. It's so wonderful to be together again, and even though I don't know what's ahead, being together right now makes me very happy.

May 1, 1986

The next morning as Mom, Laura and I drive home from physical therapy, a gardening truck hits my car and pushes it up onto the curb. I yell at the gardeners and cry, but no one speaks English. An ambulance finally arrives, not a police car, and I decide to take Laura back down to Mission Hospital. I'm worried that the sudden jolting of the car hurt her retina, but her eye is fine. The accident is minor, but it isn't what any of us needs.

Now that the brief excitement of Laura's homecoming is over, it's clear our troubles have only begun. Mom gets the flu, and Laura keeps Don and I up most of the night. The bed was wet, and she called us with tears in her eyes. After changing the sheets and blanket, we finally got back to sleep, but then the bandages on her head came off. After that, the night was almost over; Don had to be up by five for work.

As I lay in bed trying to grab those last few moments of sleep, I don't like life very much anymore. I'm tired. I want this whole ordeal to be over. We got through these horrible six weeks. Isn't that enough?

May 8

We're driving down El Toro Road. A late spring rain is coming down steadily. Don is driving; David sits next to him, and Laura and I are in the back. She has trouble keeping her balance, so I need to hold her up with my hand. The bicycle helmet covers her still bandaged head and the scars on her face are red. We're all quiet.

Suddenly Laura asks, "Mom, why did Greg save me? Why didn't you save me?"

The windshield wipers click back and forth, and I can hear the tires swishing through the thin film of water on the street. The question hangs in the silence. Don and David are both listening. I'm listening, too. For an answer to the question I've been agonizing over for weeks. I fumble an answer.

"I don't know, Laura. I just didn't know what to do. I'm so glad that Greg was there and was able to save you."

After a few seconds Don says, "This traffic is terrible. I guess it's because of the rain."

I breathe a silent thanks to him for changing the subject as I stare out the wet window, but the question, and the guilt, still hangs in my mind.

I'm back at the park, watching Laura, limp in the lion's mouth. I just stand and scream. I don't know what to do. I'm afraid. Frozen in time. I can't move. The lion will run away with her if I come closer. Nothing in my life has ever remotely prepared me for this moment. My mind is desperate, trying to think of what to do. I'm so afraid. Then it's all a blank. I remember nothing till Greg says. "Pick up your baby and get out of here."

And then, then I can move. I know what to do. I push through the cactus and lift her carefully.

The clicking of the windshield wipers brings me back to the present. I stare through the blurry drops of water on the car window. I've gone back over these moments so many times. Why didn't I save you, Laura? I love you so much. When the moment came, that moment that proves what kind of person we are, that moment we all wonder about, I stood there and did nothing.

Even Laura, young and innocent, knows that I should have saved her. I was in shock and paralyzed with fright. No one has said anything to make me feel guilty, but guilt washes over me in great waves.

May 14

One Wednesday evening the doorbell rings. An unknown lady stands smiling at the door with a steaming casserole dish. Her children smile shyly with more dishes. They ask about Laura. I answer with some stock phrases.

I thank her for the dinner. But after the screen door swings shut, I realize how flat and expressionless my 'thank you' had been, like I didn't really mean it. But I do. I'm so grateful for the help that people have given us.

I remember a picture that Laura drew last year. She sat at the kitchen table with a big white sheet of drawing paper and her crayons next to her. She colored with big red scrawls, back and forth. Then she added yellow, lots of yellow. I remember glancing at the picture as I worked in the kitchen. Green and blue, then orange, brown, some purple. Soon the paper was a brownish mush of colors, heavy with too much crayon and tearing as she added more. She pushed the paper aside, to start with a clean sheet.

My life is that bright picture of colors that turned to a brownish ugly mess. Shades of angry red at God, the county, the rangers and officials who didn't warn us. A few scrawls of yellow for the miraculous things that have gone right. And black for the moments of despair. My life has turned an ugly shade of brown.

Even though God has been absent from my life, I can't stop thinking about Him. When I watch Laura move her arm, I'm grateful, but then she tries to walk and I'm angry. Laura already knew how to walk, but now she has to learn all over again. How could He let that happen?

My feelings about God yoyo between thankful and grateful, hateful and angry. Then there's the aching thought that God had nothing to do with Laura's attack. Perhaps He didn't plan it, didn't mean it to be a test; perhaps He's not a loving father or even listening to our prayers. Perhaps He's nothing at all. That's the thought that haunts me day and night. I give lip service to God, mouthing the old words, outwardly still believing, but on the inside I feel only a vast emptiness.

Chapter 11

Laura's stuffed animals

May 23

Mike stops by on Friday morning. Luckily I'm dressed and my hair is combed as I open the door.

"I know it's early…" he apologizes.

"Come on in." I open the screen. He follows me into the kitchen and glances at the picture Laura is drawing at the kitchen table.

"Nice picture."

Laura smiles.

"Can I bother you for a cup of coffee?" He sits down next to Laura, and after I hand him his cup, stirs in some sugar.

"I found out some new information about the park," he begins. "Apparently, the rangers were so worried about the mountain lion that they contacted the county and asked them what to do about the situation."

I clear off a spot on the table and sit down. "Do you want milk?" I ask him.

"No, I'm fine. Ok, two things. Number one. The police report, you know, the one we couldn't get. The report says that there were tracks of one mountain lion at the place where Laura was attacked." He pauses and sips the coffee.

"You finally got the report? Good. Why were they so difficult about it?"

"Well, that police report had been changed."

"Changed? What do you mean?"

"Changed, as in erased, typed over. It originally said there were two mountain lions, and it was changed to read 'one.'"

"You're kidding!"

"I'm not kidding. Look at this. Right here." He points to the sentence.

"The original says clearly that there were 'two mountain lions'. Now look at the police report that we got. It says 'one lion.'

"Why would they do that?"

"Well, I think it's because, when they killed that mountain lion, they could say that the park was safe and reopen it. But now we know there's another lion out there, probably the one that attacked Laura."

I shake my head. "I can't believe this. We haven't even filed our lawsuit yet and they changed it."

"I know, but they're worried. They knew they should have done something. So they started the cover-up before we even file. Are you ready for more?"

"Yeah." I wonder what can match deliberately changing the police report.

Mike pulls out another paper. "Okay, this is what was happening in the months of February and March, right before Laura's attack. It was serious enough that the county contacted the California Department of Fish and Game and asked them what to do about the situation."

"All the groups involved—the park, the ranger, the county, the Department of Fish and Game, and the Environmental Protection Agency— decide that they need to have a meeting to talk about the mountain lion situation and find possible solutions, like closing the park or warning the public. Guess when the meeting was scheduled?"

"When?"

"March 25th, two days after Laura's attack. They canceled it as soon as they found out about the attack."

I feel like someone has punched me in the stomach. They knew there was a problem, and did nothing. The problem was enough for an emergency meeting, and yet they didn't even bother to warn us. Mike leaves quickly, and I finish cleaning the kitchen. The lawsuit has gone from the simple negligence of county employees to an actual cover-up at the highest levels of the county. I may not know much about legal things, but I know that when a jury hears about changing the police report, they'll feel the same way I do right now.

May 23

Today is Mother's Day. Don and the kids buy donuts and fix hot chocolate for my breakfast. We don't do anything special for the rest of the day. Don and I are both exhausted. But David gives me a little card and Laura has drawn hearts and written the word MOM. I hold those pieces of paper in my hand, tears in my eyes. Mother's Day has taken on new meaning, now that I almost lost one of my children.

I'm sitting on the couch, after everyone's gone to sleep, when David peeks out of his door.

"Hi sweetie. Thanks for your card today. Come and talk to me." I pat the empty seat.

He sits down next to me and slides his feet up under his Star Wars pajamas. "I can't sleep. Every time I close my eyes I see everything that happened that day."

I put my arm around him. "Yeah, I remember it all the time too."

"I was, oh, never mind."

"No, what were you going to say?" I want him to talk about that day.

"Well, when I told you that first day that everything was going to be ok, I was more wishing that. I didn't really know if it was going to be ok."

Oh, my brave little boy! I tell him, "I know, but it really helped me a lot. And everything is turning out like we hoped." I reach over and give him a big hug.

After David goes back to bed, I think about his last two months. He seems so lost. No one pays any attention to him. He sits for hours with his airplane books, drinks a lot of Dr. Pepper, and goes skateboarding with his two friends who don't seem like very good friends. They're best friends with each other, and David gets called as an afterthought, or completely forgotten.

I worry about him. I hoped so much that he would get to know my parents when they came out. It was the first time he really had the chance to spend some time with them, since they live in St. Louis. But they were strangers when they came and when they left. I don't know what I expected. He's only nine years old.

My old Irish grandfather came to stay with my parents when I was ten. I never knew what to say to him. I loved music and reading and I couldn't imagine talking to him about anything. How I later regretted not getting to know him. I wasn't old enough to realize that he had his own amazing life that he would have shared, if only I had asked. He died when I was twelve.

A few years ago, I had a dream about my grandfather. We were sitting in a circle of family members, and he was sitting right next to me. He was old and stooped over slightly, but his smile was always so tender. I turned to him, finally, and started asking him questions about his life. I wanted to know as much as I could. He opened his mouth, but he couldn't speak to me. He smiled his kind smile and turned away. I cried when I woke up. So why would I think that David could get to know my parents? It was just wishful thinking.

And then there's my relationship with Don. I read that couples who live through a traumatic event have a divorce rate somewhere around ninety percent. I hope that doesn't happen to us. I love Don, but we've hardly gone through this together. I don't mean he hasn't been here for us. He has. More than anyone could ever expect. I couldn't have gotten through the last two months without him. He's the best father, and has struggled to take care of us and work at the same time.

But we haven't been together emotionally. The only time we talk is when there's an urgent problem. I need to get things out by talking and Don holds it all inside. Our different communication styles always were a problem, and now it's just getting worse.

May 30

Most of the cash coming into the trust fund is in five and ten dollar amounts, and the addresses seem to be from the poorer places in the county and state. People in wealthy areas like Newport Beach don't send very much.

I get a five-dollar bill and a letter written with shaky handwriting that says, "I wish I could give more to that dear little girl, because I have grandchildren of my own, but I'm living on a fixed income and this is all I can give."

Another envelope contains three worn dollar bills from a small town in Tennessee. "We saved up these money and wanted to help the girl." The handwriting and spelling is poor. The note is signed by a mother and four of her children.

I would never have spoken to that lady and her family if I had met them. They would seem poor and uneducated, and I value education and intelligence. I'm such a snob. But their generosity and good hearts are what matters, not their education. It's a new and difficult lesson for me to learn.

Every night I worry that Laura might fall out of bed, hitting her head on the steel rails we've installed. I'm standing in her room trying to figure out how to make the sides softer. Everything I've tried, pillows and couch cushions, have fallen out between the rails. I notice the banana, leaning up against the wall. It looks at me with its unblinking red eyes. Perfect. I put it inside the hard rail. Now Laura is protected by the best pillow of all, the yellow banana. Who would have ever thought it would be useful?

June 7

Don and I get in a fight one Saturday morning about some unpaid bills. I run outside in tears. He's so unfair. I can't do everything. He can't either. This is too much for both of us.

My heart is pounding. I sit down in a chair by the peach tree. I feel weak and sick to my stomach.

My heart doesn't stop pounding. After a half hour I know something is very wrong. I go back inside and tell Don I have to go to the doctor. We take Laura and David over to Mike's and head for the emergency room. I feel light-headed and sick. After a long hour of waiting in the emergency room, I see a doctor. He recommends that I stay overnight so they can get my heart back to its regular beat. Don has to leave to watch the kids. Our argument is forgotten. No one is surprised that I'm in the hospital. They completely understand that it's from stress but I have to stay overnight to make sure. Mike comes to see me late that evening. I look and feel terrible and am embarrassed about it. He pulls up a chair by my bed.

"Sue, you have to get someone to help you with Laura. You have to stay healthy for her and your whole family."

I nod but don't say anything.

"I'm going to look up visiting nurses and get someone out there for you. You need someone to look after Laura for at least part of the day. You have to do this, you know."

I spend a long, lonely night in the hospital. Mike is true to his word. I get a call from the visiting nurses association and arrange for someone to come over three times a week for a few hours.

The doorbell rings the next morning. A middle-aged woman with a permanent frown is standing at the door. She comes in the house, but keeps looking around when I talk to her about Laura.

"Everything will be fine," she assures me as I walk anxiously out the front door. I'm free for three hours. I drive to the mall a few blocks away. I walk quickly into Macy's and look at the perfume and make-up. The ladies behind the counter would love to give me a free makeover with their expensive products, but I slip past them into the mall. Clothes, shoes, a new swimsuit store. I walk past all of them.

The exercise is good for me, but my mind is back home with Laura. I wonder how she's getting along with the nurse. I see a phone booth. I'm tempted to call. No, keep walking. The jewelry store is ahead. I don't need diamonds. I need time. I get all the way down to Sears at the end of the mall but I don't want anything, so I turn around and walk up the other side. Watches, pretzels, crystals.

I hope Laura's all right. What if the nurse isn't any good? She wasn't paying much attention when I talked to her. I walk faster. What if something happens? At least I'm walking. I can't find a store interesting enough to go inside. I see the kaleidoscope of colors and clothing and the people around me, but my mind is with Laura. I walk out of Macy's, get in my car and drive home.

Laura hates the grouchy nurse, so I request a different one. A young girl comes two days later and I'm even more worried. It takes fifteen minutes to explain everything to her, what Laura can and can't do. I make a quick trip to the supermarket and sit in my driveway, wasting a few more minutes. Everything is fine when I go inside. Next time will be better, because she'll know Laura and I'll trust the girl more and more.

Two days later, a new nurse comes. I have to start over again, explaining everything a third time. I put a call in to the agency. "The next nurse will be the one we keep. I can't have new people each time." So the next Monday a new nurse comes. Laura hates her and cries when I tell her the nurse will be back. I reluctantly cancel the service. No one can take care of Laura like I can. No one knows all that can go wrong.

June 16

Don's home for the weekend. I ask him to keep an eye on Laura and I walk outside to the backyard. The sky is a deep blue. A flock of Canadian geese slide through the air inches above the roof, their wings swishing through the air like tissue paper. I walk over to the side yard. Lemons hang from the tree like yellow globes; the orange tree intertwines its branches as it reaches upwards for sunlight. Usually by this time I'd be planting my garden in the soft dry dirt. I like to plant simple things: tomatoes, beans, carrots and bell peppers. Nothing grows very well, but I try every year. I love gardens, and I sit down on the plastic stool and dig out a few weeds.

The last time I planted this garden I was a different person. Everything has changed. My family, Laura, Don, my marriage. My garden inside has had too many sunless days. Too many people and responsibilities crowding in and demanding, always demanding, like weeds. Nothing is going to grow this year, that's for sure.

The last time I planted this garden it was just a garden. Now it's my life.

Chapter 12

June 24

We decide to file the lawsuit. We have the police report and the call from the lady about the trails, and Rich finally feels confident that we have a case. He flies down from San Francisco and files the paperwork. We're suing the county of Orange for an undisclosed amount for negligence.

June 27

Laura is sitting on the floor of the family room watching cartoons, her wheelchair next to her. If she needs to get up, I'll lift her into the wheelchair.

Down at the hospital, she can walk, holding on to the rails in the corridor, but we don't have anything to hold onto at home. I'm constantly afraid that she'll fall and hit that exposed area of brain. She can't wear the bicycle helmet all day. Her head is still bandaged. Her face is red and scarred across her forehead through the bridge of the nose and all across the cheek. I'm watching her watch TV, thinking of all this, when the phone rings.

"This is it, Sue! We have our case!" Mike gets right to the point, without the usual joke.

"What do you mean?"

"I got a call this morning from a lawyer named David Spangenberg. Listen to this. He and some friends and their sons went to Casper's on March 22, that Saturday. They were there all day, letting their kids play on the hillsides, not watching them very much, and later that night, they went to a ranger talk at the visitor center. Are you listening to this?"

"I'm listening, go on."

"At the talk, the ranger said something about mountain lions, and one of the dads asked if there really were mountain lions in the park, and the ranger said there was a big male that had come into the park in the last few months, and said, 'If you kids see him, stand still, don't run or he'll attack you.'"

Oh my God, I can't believe what Mike is telling me.

"Well," Mike continues, "the room was silent after that, and the meeting broke up, but Spangenberg and his friends were upset about not being told about this earlier. Spangenberg's son is in a wheelchair. In fact, he goes to Laura's school for handicapped children. The next morning the dads told their kids they couldn't play and they all decided to leave the park early, Sunday morning. Right before you came in."

I finally find my voice. "I don't understand. If it's so important to our case, why did he wait for so long to call us?"

"This is even stranger. His uncle is head of the Environmental Protection Agency, so I guess there was some loyalty to the county. And he didn't know if we were going to go ahead with the lawsuit, so he waited the ninety days till we filed. But now that we're suing the county, he decided to come forward."

"You know what this means!" Mike is excited. "If the rangers were warning people, they knew how dangerous the situation was. So they should have warned everyone. Sue, this is it. This is our case."

We talk for a few more minutes, but Mike wants to call Rich right away.

I tell Laura I'm stepping outside. The peach tree and the apricot tree have lots of green fruit on them. I hadn't even noticed that they'd blossomed. I look at the deep green leaves of the trees against the bright blue sky.

I think of the ranger sitting in his booth at the entrance to Casper's Park, and how simple it would have been for him to warn us. I don't care about the legal part. Just from one human to another. "There's a problem here that you need to know about."

They had warned other people, but not us. What cruel fate made it so that Laura would suffer her whole life for lack of a simple warning?

I sit in the white plastic chair under the peach tree and cry. I wish I could cry more, but if I do, I'll never be able to stop. I go back inside and sit down next to Laura to watch some cartoons.

I'm so impressed with Mike Madigan. When I first contacted him, I didn't even know what he did. How lucky we are to have gotten a private investigator who has thrown himself into the case with such energy and enthusiasm.

Mike does everything those first few months. He is a man with a cause. He is working full time on our case, uncovering every possible piece of evidence. He talks to the rangers, the Department of Fish and Game, the wildlife specialist at the sanctuary next to Casper's. Every day he has a new story, a new lead for the following day.

Mike helps with Laura's trust fund. He worries about the park's reopening. I find out a lot about Mike those first few months. He's done a lot of different things in his life. He operated a movie theater, worked on an import and export business in Morocco, studied opera in Italy, and thought about law, but switched to investigation. Our lawsuit is his current cause, and he's like a whirlwind in our lives.

June 28

Mike calls one afternoon. "Bring Laura and Dave over to see our new kittens. They were born yesterday. We'll fix dinner."

We drive to Mike and Carol's, who live just a few blocks away, and see the new kittens. They're so helpless, and the mother licks them as they try to nurse. Laura sits by the box all evening, watching them. A few weeks later the kittens have striped gray fur and their eyes are open. They fall over each other in the box. By now, Mike's two daughters are bored with the kittens, but Laura and David are still thrilled.

Mike invites a *Los Angeles Times* reporter to his house for an interview with Laura. The photographer takes a photo of Laura holding one of the fluffy gray kittens, and it's in the paper the next day. Mike calls the kitten "Star." Before I know what's happening, Laura is pleading with me on the short trip home. "Please Mom, can't we have Star? We love her and she's so cute, and she's almost ours anyway, cause she was in the paper with me and everything. Please?"

It doesn't matter what Don or I think at this point. Star is a member of the family.

July 3

Mike throws the *Orange County Register* down on our kitchen table.

"You want coffee?" I ask him as Don comes out of the computer room to say hello.

"No," he growls. "Look at this. There've been sightings in Casper's and we're going into the weekend of the Fourth and the park isn't warning anyone. The sightings aren't even in the paper. I'm going to go down there and warn people myself."

The reports have come to Mike from an anonymous park official. We're terrified that there will be another attack. We know that the lion is still there, most likely the one that attacked Laura. The county won't warn anyone. If they do, they'll be admitting that they should have warned us. They're afraid of our lawsuit and so they're endangering other people's lives. I can taste how much I want them to pay for their negligence. We have to win.

Don and I spend the Fourth of July at Mike's, eating ribs and steak and complaining about the county. I remember the fires on the camp stoves the day of the attack and how the people stood there in the distance, silent figures, while we ran screaming for help. I can't get the image out of my head, but the day passes without incident. Mike doesn't have much to say. What we all feared didn't happen.

"But it will," Mike says as he prepares for other interviews with park officials.

July 16

Pasta is simmering on the stove one afternoon when the doorbell rings. I yell to Dave to see who it is.

"It's Mike."

"Tell him to come in."

I don't hear anything else, so I put the pasta in the strainer and walk in the living room. The front door is open. David is out on the street with Mike, throwing a baseball. David tries to catch it with an oversized glove. Mike adjusts it for him. They try a few more balls.

"Mom, can I go down to the park and try out the bat?"

Mike walks up to the door before I can answer.

"I got him a catcher's mitt and bat. I thought he might like to play some baseball... If that's ok?"

"That's great. Thanks."

Mike has two girls who are ten and eight, and they're not interested in baseball, but David is thrilled. We start watching the games mid-season, even though the Angels aren't very good. David doesn't care. We get to know all the players on the team and David can hardly wait to try out for Little League in the fall.

I thank Mike for introducing David to baseball. He loves it, and although I know it will take its place in a long list of loves, like dinosaurs and airplanes and science experiments, I also know that David needs something to make him feel special. Laura has gotten all the attention for the last five months, and David has been left out and neglected. I'm thrilled that Mike took the time and effort to help.

I'm still on that roller coaster of feelings. I see Laura with her brace, her scars, her helmet, and I'm just overwhelmed by sadness. Other times, I hear her laugh or play with Kelli, the little girl next door, and I'm so happy she's alive and doing well.

I think about the attack every day, almost every hour. It's in my dreams. I startle easily, from the slightest sound.

And then there's the guilt. It's impossible to put behind me. My whole life seemed like a preparation for one moment. Could I be courageous and strong? And when the moment came, I failed. I watched my own daughter in the jaws of a lion, and I did nothing. Why didn't I grab the branch and fight the lion? Why did it have to be a stranger who saved her?

I'm not courageous. I'm not a hero. I couldn't even save my own child. The moment has come and gone. And I failed miserably. I'll do anything for her, to make up for it. But nothing will ever be enough. How can anyone understand this?

Don tries to make me feel better.

"You couldn't have helped her. You were in a state of shock."

But I could have done something and I didn't. I can't shake the feeling of failure. It settles like a black pall over my life.

Chapter 13

Laura and David

September 4

Baroque music wakes me suddenly and I open my eyes to darkness. I hit the alarm quickly before it wakes Don. It's 4 am on a cool September morning, the first day of school. But Laura won't be going to school. She has another operation at Estelle Doheny Eye Hospital in Los Angeles. It's a fairly simple procedure to remove the oil from her eye. Doctors injected the oil a few months ago to press against the retina and help it reattach to the back of the eye. This is her last chance to regain sight in that eye.

After I throw my clothes on in the dark, I wake Laura up just enough to get her out to the car. Don gives us a kiss goodbye, but David is still asleep. I stop at his room, and look up at him in his bunk bed, his arm flung out to the side, his hair tousled. I feel bad that I'll miss his first day of fourth grade.

His face looks chubby. He's gained weight from all the snacks and soft drinks at the hospital. He was so bored that he'd go to the cafeteria or snack machine almost every day. And since we've been home, we've been eating meals and desserts that other people have prepared for us. I need to fix healthier meals. We've all gotten into bad habits.

I wish I could spend more time with David. He loves baseball now because of Mike's influence. He has a good and kind soul; he doesn't care for school, but loves to learn. He sucks in knowledge like a sponge, if he's interested. I love having him around. He's easy and happy and I always know what he's thinking because he is always talking. I hope he doesn't become a sullen teenager. I take a last look at him. I want to spend more time with him, but there just isn't any more time.

A few minutes later, I pull onto the freeway, watching the sky turn grey. An hour and a half later we pass the Los Angeles city limits. I hate driving, and it gives me a sick feeling, but maybe it's combined with worry about Laura's operation. Fortunately, Laura sleeps most of the way. We drive into the underground parking lot as the sun is coming up. We're shown to

Laura's room, and get her dressed in a hospital gown. She watches cartoons and I stare out the window at the dirty parking lot below. The ugly beige building across the street almost disappears in the thick brown smog.

The hospital pediatrician asks some questions about Laura's health, and as he turns to leave, I remember something.

"Oh, doctor, I've noticed some bruises. I know she has lots on her knees and legs, and that's normal, but look at these on her back. There's even a few on the side of her face. I don't know where she could have gotten these."

Laura has a ring of large bruises on her back, and four on the side of her face by her eye. The pediatrician looks at Laura's back and face and then smiles.

"Kids certainly do get a lot of bruises. Nothing to worry about. Well, I'll be stopping in later today to see how she's doing."

I feel silly for having brought it up. It's obviously not important.

The attendants come with the stretcher, and take Laura to the operating room. I hold her hand and give her a kiss, then they roll the stretcher through the double doors and I'm left outside.

Upstairs, I arrange her bed and plump up the unused flat pillow. The cars pull into the parking lot, one at a time. I read a few pages of a book that doesn't hold my interest, and look out the window again. It's only 8 am but the lot's almost full. The morning passes slowly. I read fitfully and stare out the window. By noon I'm beginning to worry. Cars are leaving the parking lot for lunch. I tell the nurse I'll be in the cafeteria. My food is in front of me on a plastic tray, lukewarm, when the surgeon walks up and pulls up a chair.

"Laura's fine. The operation went ok and she's in recovery right now. Actually, there was a lot of hemorrhaging in the eye, much more than usual, but I don't think it will affect the success of the operation. The retina looks good right now."

I'm filled with hope. Maybe she really will be able to see out of that eye again. That would be such a gift. But I can't help asking, "Why was there so much bleeding?"

"I don't know. Has Laura ever had any trouble with bleeding?"

"No, not at all."

"Well, I don't think it'll have any adverse effects. The next few months will be critical for keeping the retina attached. And there's the possibility, we've spoken of it before, that the cornea can become cloudy and opaque as a result of this oil implant. We'll just have to wait and see. Finish your lunch. Laura will be in the recovery room for at least an hour. We'll let you know when she's coming up."

"Thank you so much."

This doctor is one of the best eye surgeons in the city of Los Angeles. Whatever caused the bleeding doesn't concern me. The retina is attached. If the retina becomes detached from the back of the eye, it will result in total blindness.

After lunch, I go upstairs and call Don. He says he'll miss us till we get home. I wait. The cars are all back from lunch and the afternoon passes even more slowly than the morning. I ask the nurse every fifteen minutes if Laura is coming up from recovery, but the answer is always, "No, not yet. She's fine. She's just taking a long time to wake up from the anesthetic. Don't worry."

By four o'clock the sun is starting to make shadows on the buildings across the street. Finally a nurse asks me to go to the recovery room and help wake her up. She is lying quietly with her little pink bunny. Her eye is patched and she's covered with a white sheet.

"Laura, it's mom. It's over, honey, the operation is over and you did great."

But she won't wake up. She opens her eyes for a few seconds and then she drifts back to sleep. They send me back upstairs. I don't want to leave, but her vital signs are good. The nurse says, "Well, sometimes it takes longer for them to wake up."

The cars are all gone now and the parking lot is in shadows. The operation was over before noon and Laura doesn't get out of recovery until eight that night. Just in time to go to sleep.

I call Don, and tell him about the operation. He says if the doctors aren't worried, then he isn't either. I worry all night, though, because with the bleeding and the long time in recovery, I feel there's something wrong. But I'm assured that she's absolutely fine. Laura is much better the next day, but she has to stay another day. I can hardly wait till we get out of the hospital.

Three days is an eternity away from home. Laura seems fine the next day, a little tired, and we drive home in the afternoon.

But I still worry. About what's out there, waiting to pounce.

September 15

Laura can finally start school. She's in a special day class at R.H. Dana for the multiple handicapped. Dana Point is one of the beach cities south of Laguna Beach.

I take Laura to school the first few days so she doesn't have to ride the bus. Her teacher is young and enthusiastic, and the classroom is well equipped with large bright posters, an terrarium with a real tarantula, computers, and a small eating area. She goes to the regular kindergarten every afternoon for an hour to get used to a regular classroom.

Laura's cousin has muscular dystrophy, and he's the only handicapped child I've known. I watch the six children in the classroom, each with a lifetime of struggle ahead of them. They'll have emotional and physical problems their whole lives, and now Laura is one of them. She wears her bicycle helmet; she no longer has her head bandaged, and her hair is just starting to grow back, covering some of the red streaks that crisscross her head. The scarring on her face looks better than it did a few months ago, but it's still red and noticeable.

My day consists of taking her to school, driving the half hour back home, wandering around the house worrying about her, eating lunch, and then heading back to pick her up. After about a week I let Laura take the school bus. It's a small school bus just for the Dana students, but I worry anyway. It hurts me to see her strapped into the seat for the long ride to school, not just with a seat belt, but with a harness. But it's silly to take her when the county provides a bus.

I have more time now that Laura's in school, but I don't quite know what to do with it. I feel like I'm on the sidelines of my life, watching Laura recover, watching the lawsuit progress. I'm just watching and waiting.

September 27

When I walked into Laura's room last night, she was lying on her back with her hands folded. I realized how fragile life is. She lies there, alive and breathing, able to laugh and play, when she should have been dead. I got on my knees and thanked God.

I don't know if He's there, but if He is, I should thank Him. He seems to have no regard for us. He lets people suffer and die so senselessly, so randomly. It has nothing to do with our sins, or our guilt. He is so silent, so uninvolved. We are born and we don't know why. We live an entire lifetime not knowing any answers. Is there life after death? Why was I born? Why do tragic things happen? Why do people die? And there are no answers. Oh, for a few who believe there are answers. But what about most people, drifting aimlessly through life? Why does He ignore us? Why is he so far away?

And why must I guess that it was God who helped Laura? Was it pure chance that she was attacked but not killed?

Or was he there, with his hand over her, so that she didn't die? I want to know. Is that too much to ask?

Sometimes I think life is a classroom. We wake up and we're all in a huge classroom, with no teacher. The doors are locked. We wonder what we're supposed to be studying, why we're there, and what will happen if we pass or fail the class. We call out repeatedly for the teacher, but he or she never comes. We're on our own. We stumble and muddle through random books left in the classroom, not knowing or understanding anything. We share what we know and what we've read, but the teacher never shows up. Is God like that, leaving us in this classroom alone for our whole lives, with no answers?

I want to find out the answers for myself. I've had them handed to me my whole life, and now I don't know if they're right or wrong. So this time I go alone, on my own path. I hope it leads to Him. If He's there, it will.

October 1

Laura's school calls and says she isn't feeling well. She can't seem to shake a slight cold. She's tired and pale and isn't eating much. The bruises are still there, on her face and upper arm and back. I pick her up and stop by Dr. Shannon's on the way home, just to make sure.

Dr. Shannon looks at the bruises carefully.

"I'd like to get a blood test, just to see about this bruising." He doesn't dismiss it like the other doctor. But he smiles his big warm smile and laughs with Laura, and I'm not worried.

Later that day Dr. Shannon calls. Laura's blood test results are low, not dangerously low, but enough to be of concern. After consulting with a pediatric neurologist, he suggests we take Laura off the phenobarbitol, because sometimes that drug can lower the blood count.

"What about the chance of a seizure?" Laura has never had a seizure, but her brain scans are abnormal. That's why the doctors put her on Phenobarbital, just as a precaution.

"Well, phenobarbitol stays in the blood for a while, and we'll get a brain scan at UCI to see if she even needs it anymore. Then we'll have another blood test to see if that's really the problem."

October 13

Laura has been off her medication for two weeks when we go for a second blood test. She doesn't feel like playing with the toys in Dr. Shannon's office, but luckily the nurse calls us in right away. We walk past a whole roomful of waiting mothers and children. I lift Laura up on the examination table as Dr. Shannon comes to the door. He's not smiling. The blood test results are much lower. Her platelets, which should normally be around 200,000, are 32,000. The red and white blood cell counts are also dangerously low.

"We're very fortunate to have an excellent hematologist right here in the same building. I've already called him to take a look at Laura's blood count. I've set up an appointment for tomorrow morning at the hospital."

The next morning Don comes with us, and we say hi to all the nurses in pediatrics. They gather around Laura, happy to see her doing so well. A small, dark haired man walks quickly toward us. "Hello, I'm Dr. Cairo. Let's just go in this room."

Don and I leave Laura with the nurses and walk into the empty exam room. After a few seconds, Dr. Cairo takes a deep breath and says, "I know that you've been through a lot in the past few months, and I hate to be the bearer of bad news, but Laura's blood count is extremely low. I'd like to take a bone marrow sample right now so that I can look at it. Then we'll talk further."

Don and I numbly agree. Dr. Cairo sounds worried, but it's hard to judge a doctor the first time he speaks. Some of them stress the positive, others the negative. Maybe the worry in his voice is just his style, like Dr. Palmer.

We go into the narrow procedure room with Laura, but the nurse asks us to leave.

"A bone marrow aspiration is a difficult procedure and it's better if the parents aren't here," she says with a smile. So Don and I stand out quietly in the hall.

It's nothing to worry about, I tell myself over and over again. It's the phenobarbital, just like Dr. Shannon says, and we can easily change the medication. Dr.

Cairo is just being cautious, especially after all she's been through.

And then I hear Laura scream. I jump up and tell the nurse I want to go inside the room. "No," she says firmly. A bone marrow aspiration, I discover, is extremely painful. Even though the area is anesthetized, a large needle has to be pushed into the back, down to the pelvic bone and into the center of the bone, to get a sample of bone marrow. I'm angry at myself that we didn't stay with her.

As soon as the door opens, we walk in quickly and hold Laura as she cries. She is so brave, I can't imagine how much this procedure hurt. As Dr. Cairo leaves the room, he turns around, "Does Laura have any brothers or sisters?"

"Yes, she has a brother."

I have an ominous feeling. That's the question asked about a donor for a bone marrow transplant. But I just as quickly put the idea out of my mind. There could be other reasons why he would ask that question. I always jump to conclusions. My little knowledge of medicine is dangerous. Don and I sit quietly in the waiting room with Laura as she talks to one of her old nurses, her tears finally drying.

Another nurse leans into the doorway. "Dr. Cairo would like to see you in room 102."

We leave Laura with the nurse, and walk into the empty room. A white sheet lies flat and tight on the small bed with no pillow, and the bare walls and antiseptic black and white tile floor give me a sudden feeling of sadness. Dr. Cairo walks in and looks at the floor.

"I'm really very sorry, but your daughter has a disease we call aplastic anemia. It's an extremely low blood count. The white blood cells, the red blood cells and the platelets are no longer being produced by the bone marrow."

I listen in disbelief, picking up the sadness and resignation in his voice. But there's no need. Doesn't he understand? We've gone through the horrible part. Laura is getting better. I force myself to listen.

"Most of the time we don't ever know the cause of the disease. In Laura's case it's an allergic reaction to a drug called chloramphenicol, which she was given here at this hospital in March."

A thousand thoughts spin through my head. He's wrong. I mean, he doesn't know the whole story. Laura's fine. The worst is over. She's doing so well. Her eye is very bad, we know that, the recovery from the paralysis is slow, but she's improving. It isn't possible that anything else could go wrong. Especially something so hidden, so unknown.

Dr. Cairo continues, "There's nothing we can do for aplastic anemia. I'd like to have her admitted to CHOC, Children's Hospital of Orange County, for a few days, so we can monitor her blood levels constantly. And I want both of you and your son to get HLA testing for a possible bone marrow match in case she needs a bone marrow transplant."

A bone marrow transplant? My heart is frozen with fear. I don't know anything about aplastic anemia, but I know that a bone marrow transplant is a life threatening procedure, used when all else fails.

She still could die. My heart cries out weakly at the unfairness of it.

But there's nothing I can do except stand helplessly, my arms reaching out to her as she is attacked. And again I'm too late, as she is grabbed and dragged away, this time by an invisible beast.

Chapter 14

October 16

We pack Laura's bag and drive up to Children's Hospital the next morning. David goes with us to get his blood tested. He's not happy about the blood test, but he's thrilled about missing school.

We arrive at ten, because our blood has to be taken early so it can be sent out before two o'clock. We wait for over an hour in the waiting area. I start reminding the receptionist every ten minutes that we're there, but after the third time, she rolls her eyes and says we have to wait our turn. Close to noon we wonder how long we have to keep waiting. I check with the receptionist and remind her that the blood needs to be out soon. She looks up but looks past me. She is quite aware of that, she informs me.

We're all hungry and Laura isn't feeling too well to begin with. At one o'clock the nurse finally calls us. She throws me a parting glance that seems to say, "You thought you were special, but see, you had to wait just like everybody else!"

Laura screams when they take her blood. It's not her first blood test, but the technicians have to take so many vials, one after another, that I lose count and look away. We all give more blood than we've ever given before. David tries to be brave, but I see a few tears slide down his face. Finally we're finished and we can get Laura admitted to the hospital.

Laura's in a large ward with three other girls. A four-year old has a large plastic tube in her chest so the technicians can take blood more easily. Another teenager is bald from chemotherapy treatments, but wears a pink ribbon around her head and smiles at us. Each family keeps to itself, careful not to intrude.

Laura is tired and bored. She gets a late hospital lunch and the rest of us find a McDonalds. When we get back to the hospital a technician walks in Laura's room and tells us we have to redo all our lab work. He explains that the blood samples had to be out by two o'clock and that ours were taken too late.

"We got here at ten this morning and it took them three hours to get the blood samples. It's not our fault they have to be redone." I'm so angry I can hardly speak.

He shrugs his shoulders. The blood tests have to be redone. I let him redo Laura's but I refuse to have ours done there. We'll go down to Mission Hospital the next morning.

Don and David go home, and I lie on a cot by Laura's bed that night, and listen to a girl cry quietly in the corner bed. I wish I could help her, but there's nothing I can do. My prayers are desperate. "I hope You're really there. I'm sorry if I've ever doubted You. I'll do anything, anything, so that Laura will be alright."

But even though I want to appease God, I can't understand how he can let this happen. The mountain lion attack, I'm willing to concede, wasn't entirely in his hands. The negligence of the county had been the real reason for the attack. Maybe God does clean-up work for what humans do badly. That seems sensible, since most wars and tragedies are caused by human greed and a lust for power. But this aplastic anemia didn't have to happen. It's a one in forty thousand reaction to this particular drug. God could have prevented this. And the girl crying in the corner bed, her hair gone and her body ravaged by cancer. Where is God for her?

In the dim light I open my old convent Bible and read the words of St. Paul, who seems to understand.

"We are subjected to every kind of hardship, but are never distressed; we see no way out, but we never despair; we are pursued, but never cut off; knocked down, but still have some life in us."

Listening to other children through the night, I struggle with questions that have no answers. These children have not been abused by parents, or hurt by someone's negligence. All these children have cancer or other blood diseases, their suffering and sickness perhaps not caused by God, but certainly allowed by Him. And why? For what possible reason?

I wake up self-consciously in the morning, brushing my hair back hastily and straightening my wrinkled, slept-in clothes, as nurses and technicians come into the room.

After I quickly splash my face with water and brush my teeth in the tiny restroom, Dr. Cairo makes his rounds. He wants to do another bone marrow aspiration and we still have to repeat our blood tests at

Mission. After he leaves, Laura picks at her breakfast. A technician in a white coat comes in with empty test tubes. He walks up to Laura's bed.

"Good morning," he says brightly.

"No, you're not going to take her blood." I put my hand out, pushing him away.

He stops with the rubber tubing in mid-air. "This is just a routine blood sample. We take these every morning."

"Do you have a specific order from Dr. Cairo?"

"Well, no ma'am, I don't." He looks down at me and smiles.

"Well, you can't take any blood till you have a direct order from him."

He shakes his head, and moves on to the next bed.

This is so unlike me, telling this man what to do, but I've finally reached the point where I don't care what anyone thinks. Laura's blood is in terrible shape. She gave blood three days ago. She had a bone marrow aspiration and a blood sample the next day and yesterday she had a lot of blood drawn for the bone marrow tests. She doesn't have much left to give. None of us do.

Dr. Cairo schedules another bone marrow aspiration for the afternoon. I try out my new attitude and tell the nurse I'm going to stay with Laura.

She looks above me at the wall. "We prefer for the parents to be out of the room. It's very crowded and we don't want people fainting."

"I've seen worse, and I'm going to stay with Laura."

The nurse in charge finally looks at me. "Ok."

I hold Laura's hand while they anesthetize the area and force the long wide needle into her back until it reaches the bone. I hold Laura's hand tightly, and she smiles at me through the tears.

I'm helpless, but at least I'm there. I will never stay away again because somebody tells me. I can't do anything, but I'm with her and care about her and that's important.

October 19, 1986

When the results come back from the blood tests, it turns out that Don and I are only half matches. But David is a perfect match.

The next day's test shows the platelets up from 32,000 to 70,000. Dr. Cairo decides to wait and watch her blood count carefully. When Rich, our lawyer, hears about Laura's aplastic anemia, and the implication that the antibiotic chloramphenicol caused it, he goes to the medical library in San Francisco and does some research.

Laura's blood count climbs a little higher every day, and Dr. Cairo comes in one morning. He stands confidently in front of me. "I think I definitely did the right thing." He pauses. "Which was nothing. But it was absolutely the correct decision."

I shake his hand. It sounds funny, that he's so pleased with himself for having done nothing. After I think about it during the day, I realize that if he was more aggressive and ordered a bone marrow transplant, she could have easily died. Yes, I am so grateful that he did nothing.

Laura comes home from the hospital, still exhausted, and now has a weekly blood test in addition to the therapy.

Rich calls back with the results of his research.

"We have to sue the doctors that prescribed chloramphenicol for Laura. They knew that drug had a high risk of blood problems. I want to do some further research."

I shake my head even though he can't see it. "I'm not going to sue the doctors. Dr. Palmer told me that chloramphenicol was the best antibiotic because it could penetrate the brain. We didn't want her to get a brain infection and die."

"Well, they knew the risks that were involved and shouldn't have taken that chance." Rich is really angry.

"You can do all the research you want, but I'm not suing the doctors. Laura would be dead without them."

"Listen, you don't know what I've found out about this. Aplastic anemia is a deadly disease. The rate of spontaneous recovery is only about three percent. It looks like Laura is one of the lucky three percent, so I think she's going to be fine. But Sue, three percent recovery rate!"

"Are you sure about that?"

"I've got it right in front of me. I'll bring this down next week."

We say goodbye and I put down the phone. I feel like another bullet has whizzed by, barely missing Laura. I don't want to sue any doctors. That I know for sure. I think of their faces, compassionate, caring; the time they gave to her, the effort they put into saving her life. Sue them? Rich is crazy if he thinks we're going to do that.

Three percent recovery. Yes, I should be thankful to God that she is recovering, but why did she get aplastic anemia in the first place? God gets all the credit when something good happens, but none of the blame for the bad things. How many times have I read about horrific car accidents, seven dead, and the one miracle person that God saved. Why is that? Why do we think of God only when the good things happen? I'm responsible, whether I like it or not, for everything I've done, the good and the bad. Why isn't God?

As Laura and I leave the hospital, we walk past rooms filled with children. Most on this floor have no hair. Some are sleeping; others have families with them. Balloons and stuffed animals are in all the rooms, and flowers and toys. But there are so many children who will never get to go home. The toys and flowers and stuffed animals make no difference in the end. And Who takes the blame for that?

Chapter 15

Lion, watching family at Caspers

October 26

Linda schedules a choir meeting for Sunday. I want to get back to choir, away from the constant worry. I want to escape from my life, but it's increasingly difficult. Anytime I think about Laura's medical condition, my family, or the lawsuit, I'm confronted with problems that don't have solutions.

Mike and I go to the choir meeting in his Rolls Royce. He's been increasingly active in the choir. He has an excellent bass voice and is interested in helping with the choir finances. We're sitting at the meeting and I'm almost feeling back to normal, when the phone rings in the next room. Someone jumps up and answers it, then comes into the living room.

"Sue, it's for you."

My heart practically stops. Something's happened to Laura. I walk quickly in the kitchen and grab the phone.

"Sue, it's me, Don. I just got a phone call from the *Los Angeles Times*. A little boy got attacked at Casper's today."

"Oh, God. Is he ok?"

"The man from the Times didn't know. He was on his way down to Mission."

"I'll come home right away." I hang up the phone and walk into the other room.

I ignore the other people. "Mike, a little boy was attacked at Caspers. We'd better go."

Mike grabs his keys as he stands up. His choir papers flutter to the floor. Mike says nothing for the short drive home. I glance at him a few times.

"I'll see you at the hospital," he says as I step out of the car.

I knew the lion killed on March 24th wasn't the right lion. From the first moment I had seen the dead lion on the news, I knew it was the wrong animal.

I wanted the authorities to measure the size of the mouth and see if the bite marks corresponded to Laura's head wounds. The body of the mountain lion was in a freezer somewhere in Orange County, but the county wasn't interested in what I thought. They knew another mountain lion was still there.

At Mission Hospital, Don and I meet the distraught parents of Justin Mellon, the little boy who's been attacked.

They had been on the same trail we were on six months earlier, the Bell Canyon Trail. Justin bent down to tie his shoes and the rest of the party went on ahead of him. A lion grabbed him by the head and started to drag him down an embankment. His father ran back and beat off the mountain lion. Justin's injuries are not as severe as Laura's. He needs about ten stitches and stays in the hospital for a few days.

November 1

The next Saturday, we get an early morning phone call from Mike.

"Can I come over right now?"

"Uh, come on over. It's fine."

He hangs up abruptly and I'm holding a dead phone.

I'm in jeans and an old red shirt, ready to do some weeding, Don's in the computer room, and the kids are still asleep. Mike bursts into the house a few minutes later with a big color poster. I call Don from the other room. Mike leans the picture up against the living room wall and stands next to it proudly. The photo is of a woman holding a baby, surrounded by chaparral and high weeds.

"This is the Bell Canyon trail, where Laura was attacked. The woman's husband took the picture." He waits expectantly.

I look at the picture, and back at Mike. It's a nice picture, but I don't know them. And why does Mike have it? I look at Mike. He waits.

"So, who are these people?"

"Look again."

He points to a spot in the tall brown grass just behind and to the side of the woman. I can see it now. It's the head of a mountain lion; the eyes focused on the woman and her baby. It can't be more than a few feet behind the woman, but it's practically invisible in the tall brown grass.

"This picture was taken the day before Justin's attack on the Bell Canyon trail. Doug Schulthess and his wife are really nice people, I met them earlier today when they gave me a copy of the picture. They didn't even know the lion was there until they had the picture developed. Then they saw it and just panicked. Called the park to tell them and to show them the picture, but nobody at the park was interested. So they called the *LA Times*, who were very interested, and the picture will be in tomorrow's paper, on the front page."

Don and I stare at the photo.

"Oh, Mike, this will help our case so much." I can just imagine a jury's reaction to the picture.

"Well, it could. Except for one thing. This took place *after* Laura's attack, so we can't use it. Everything, the Fourth of July, Justin's attack, and this picture; none of it can be used as evidence. It's only what happened on or before March 23rd."

Somehow that seems terribly unfair. Mike takes the poster with him, but I ask him to make a copy for us. If only we could get to a trial and use that picture, I'm sure we would win.

November 6, 1986

We're standing in the living room of Grandpa Harry's house in San Luis Obispo. He had a stroke two days ago and just got home from the hospital. He's only 65 years old. He sits in the recliner by the window, unshaven and confused. He tries to get out of the chair to greet us. Tears come to his eyes.

Laura limps over to him. "Grandpa, I couldn't speak either when I was in the hospital, but I worked at it and it got a lot better. I think you'll get better, too."

I'm so proud of her. Harry seems to understand. Tears glisten in his eyes.

Don lost his mother to cancer when she was fifty-six years old. I had known Don's parents for only two years before Virginia died.

His mother was a happy, vivacious woman. She was a Christian Scientist, and believed in God and the power of prayer. She wanted to read more books, explore the California wetlands, and go clamming more in the ocean. She loved life. She wanted to do so much. Life was just beginning for her when it ended.

And then Harry met a blonde named Joanie who laughed a lot and drank even more. It was easy to see why Harry was attracted to Joanie. She was fun after Virginia's long bout with cancer and her death.

But by now, Joanie and Harry were arguing constantly, and the big fake diamonds that covered her hands are tarnished and old. She told me after their marriage that Harry was her seventh husband.

Joanie bustles around cleaning and telling us how difficult everything is. She doesn't pay much attention to Harry. No one has tried to give him a pen to see if he can write. Laura wears her pink bonnet on her head to cover the scars and is tired all weekend.

Harry shuffles around the house and is unable to say a word, and I know he doesn't want us to leave. But we must. Don has to work, David has to go to school, and Laura needs her critical blood tests. It's hard to leave him. But we must. I wonder if Joanie will leave too. I wonder if she will be any help to him at all, even if she stays.

November 20, 1986

I throw the *Los Angeles Times* on the couch with tears in my eyes. The letters to the editor are all about our case. "Why did that mother let her child wander alone in the park?" Another one says, "If you keep your children close to you and properly supervised, nothing bad will happen to them."

Don't they realize that Laura was only five feet away from me at the time of the attack? If I had more than two seconds, I could have reached out and grabbed her. But the attack was so fast I didn't even have time to do that. I saw the lion running toward her and grab her head. Then it's blank until I looked around me and felt the complete silence.

The letters say that if I had been with her this never would have happened. The county keeps repeating the same question, "Where was the mother?" because they want me to be responsible. If they can prove Laura's injuries are the result of my negligence, then they won't have to pay.

I close my eyes and remember the tawny body as it slid towards Laura. Being so close I could have touched it. Reaching out just a second too late.

I decide, crumpling up the newspaper and pushing it into the trash, to only care about the opinions of people who care about us. I can't live my life based on what some strangers think. But it still hurts.

November 30

Laura needs a corneal transplant. The cornea has become cloudy and opaque. The doctors warned us that it could happen. Dr. Robin, the corneal transplant specialist, says that if Laura were his child he would definitely go ahead with the operation. It's not without risk, but if rejection occurs, they can just do another transplant.

We wait for a donor between the ages of ten and twenty. The call will probably come within the month. The thought makes me shiver. To know that there is a young child somewhere out there who is looking forward to Christmas, bought all their presents, has a family and loved ones. Someone out there has a future they dream about, and, sometime in the next few weeks, with no warning, they will die. The family will donate the organs, and the cornea will be given to Laura so she might be able to see again. It hardly seems fair, that Laura will only have the chance to see again if someone else dies. But of course there is no "fair" anymore. I've learned that much.

December 3, 1986

Harry developed a high fever and died this evening. He was only sixty-five years old.

I'll miss going up to Arroyo Grande and seeing him. Strong, working around the house. Mowing the lawn on his tractor and taking Laura for rides. Doing that little silly dance for Laura to make her laugh. Letting her comb his hair. Always having frosted oatmeal cookies and M&M's for all of us. I'll miss how he called Laura a "little rascal," and how much he loved David and was so proud of him.

I'll miss how he loved Warren. Warren is Don's nephew and has muscular dystrophy. Now Warren has no one who will take care of him. Harry worried about Warren so much. He took care of him as long as he could, but Warren, at age 23, got too heavy for Harry to lift in and out of the wheelchair, and they had to put him in a home. I guess we'll be taking care of Warren now.

And he loved Don. He never talked about it, but you could see the pride in his eyes when his son was with him. Don could solve any problem. It seems strange that it's all part of the past now.

I look out the window to the warm December day. The sun is still shining, because it always shines in Southern California. But it means nothing. What a horrible, dark year. I'll be so glad when it's over.

We drive to San Luis Obispo for the funeral. We file into the funeral home chapel with its fake stained glass windows and dark wooden pews. Laura is crying. A few neighbors sit across the aisle. Joanie wears black with a wide blank smile.

The hired minister reads a short biography of Harry and a few prayers are recited from the book. The casket is closed. The minister forgets Harry's name and has to look at the card. I want the minister at my funeral to know who I am. The smell of lilies cloys the air. All too quickly, it's over. We drive back to the empty house where Joanie has drinks and snacks and plays the bereaved hostess.

Both of Don's parents are gone. I was so envious when we first got married. His parents were twenty years younger than mine and I felt cheated that mine were so elderly. Now I know that death is random and senseless. My parents are both alive and Don's are gone.

We don't stay too long at the house. Joanie is furious about Harry's will, which leaves his money to his two children. He leaves the house to her, but she is still angry. The strangest thing is that no one cares. We all have other things to worry about.

December 24

We're back home for Christmas. The kids and I find a last minute tree at Home Depot and decorate it with all our fun ornaments. Star Wars cruisers are strategically placed for battle around the tree. A knitted doghouse from a friend of Mom's, paper school ornaments from David and Laura, and a Hershey's cocoa ornament for me. I love our tree. Every decoration has a story. David and Laura go with me to

Midnight Mass. People surround us, and I tell everyone how well we're all doing. When we walk in the church, the choir is singing carols and pine trees line the altar with twinkling white lights. Laura sits close to me and almost falls asleep while David fidgets, and the service ends with the choir's glorious "Joy to the World."

When we get home, Don is already asleep. The kids and I celebrate quietly with hot chocolate and Christmas cookies, and they reluctantly go to bed. I curl up on the couch with my hot chocolate and listen to Christmas carols quietly on the radio, not quite ready to say goodbye to this Christmas Eve.

I think about my first Christmas in the convent, back in St. Louis, when belief made sense and the world seemed simple. The motherhouse was on a bluff overlooking the Mississippi River, and on Christmas Eve we were all sent to bed at six p.m. so we could get up for Midnight Mass. Sister Miriam, our postulant mistress, was apoplectic that one of us would get sick from lack of sleep.

On the way upstairs to our dorm, I whispered to Joanne, "Do you want to go out on the roof?" She nodded. I knew a way to get there.

We slowed down and let everyone pass us. Then we sneaked down the empty corridors to the bell tower. I stopped at a cleaning closet where I knew there was a small flashlight. The small bell tower door wasn't locked, so we slid in and closed it carefully behind us. The dust flew and we didn't dare turn on the one light bulb far above. That would announce our presence almost as much as ringing the Angelus bell. I went first, up the thin wooden circular steps that wound around the thick bell rope. I wedged the flashlight between my body and arm, and held my wool skirts up with the other hand. I needed another hand for holding the pole in the middle, but I didn't have one. I didn't dare fall. Joanne followed, cursing in the darkness. I almost slipped on a thin step, and grabbed the narrow pole right next to the rope. The flashlight almost slipped and fell. Cold sweat dripped off me as I realized I had been less than an inch away from ringing the bell.

Finally, I pushed open the trapdoor, climbed out on the roof, and wedged the door open with a leftover piece of wood.

We stood on the gently sloping roof, holding on to the ventilation pipes so we wouldn't slip on the ice and snow. It was quiet; the low clouds muffled any noise from the city. We could see far down the river; a barge flickered its red and green Christmas lights through the falling snow. The lights of the neighborhood houses twinkled in the distance until the fog swallowed them one by one.

The world was silent, like the "Silent Night" of a century ago. We stood shivering, but neither one of us turned to go back inside. We didn't say anything, just watched the world, quietly. Then Joanne saw a flake of snow land on her black sleeve and laughed in delight. She was from the central valley in California and had never seen snow.

I could barely see the snowflakes as they landed on our black habits and quickly disappeared. My nose was numb, and Joanne was starting to shake. But I caught a last look at the wintry river, the ghostlike trees standing guard at its side, and the snow peacefully dancing in the dim light. I would always remember my first Christmas away from home.

Silent Night ends on the radio, and suddenly I'm back in the present. Christmas will be a good day, and I hope with all my heart that next year will be better.

Chapter 16

Laura and her grandfather

January 5, 1987

The call about the corneal transplant comes the first week of January. We drive to UCLA and Don and I wait in Laura's room for hours. Don reads and I stare out the dirty window to a sea of parking structures. This seems to be my life now-staring out windows at rows of cars.

Dr. Robin walks in five hours later. He looks exhausted. 'Well, I'm sorry to tell you this, but even though the corneal transplant was successful, the retina pulled away completely from the back of the eye. There was just too much scar tissue. We can't save the eye." We talk a few more minutes, but there's nothing more to be said.

"The nurse will come for you when Laura starts to wake up. She'll take you down to the recovery room."

Don and I sit quietly after Dr. Robin leaves the room.

I speak first. "All those months, and all the hard work to save the eye, and it's over, just like that."

"I know," Don says, "I feel terrible."

"What's she going to do? What if something happens to her other eye?" I start to cry.

"A lot of people do fine with just one eye."

"I'm just worried."

"Yeah, I know." Don stares out the window.

A nurse comes to the door. "I can take you down to the recovery room now."

Don and I go down the elevator with the nurse. I paste a smile on my face and walk in to see Laura. She is tired, but smiles at us. I look at her patched eye and hope the future will be brighter for her than it seems right now.

January 15, 1987

David and I are sitting at the kitchen table eating breakfast. He jumps up. "The cat. It has a bird!" He slides open the back door and rushes outside. I run after him.

Sylbuster, our black cat, slinks up the slope to the pine trees. Something is in his mouth. David runs after him, trying to grab the cat with his outstretched hands. I stand, staring at the cat and bird, feeling a wave of nausea. I can't think. I have to get the bird away from the cat.

I run up beside David, trying to grab the cat. I have to save the bird. My heart knows that feeling of terror, of hopelessness, of rage. I know what to do this time. I grab for the cat, but he leaps away and runs down the sidewalk.

With my legs shaking, I run after him. I can see the bird fluttering weakly in the cat's mouth. Sylbuster's sleek black body jumps up on the fence and disappears into the neighbor's yard.

Tears are streaming down David's face. It's the first time I've seen him cry since Laura's attack. There's nothing to say. We've already lived through this; the cruelty of nature, the survival of the fittest, and the randomness of the universe.

I take David to school, and neither of us ever talks about the incident again. But the intensity of my reaction scares me. I wonder what other emotions are below the surface, waiting to explode.

January 20, 1987

The kids are both asleep. I turn on the TV and start flipping channels.

"Can we talk for a second?" Don comes over to the couch ad sits down.

Don never wants to talk. I turn off the TV.

"I'm going to start seeing Dr. Jacobs for my depression. I started last week and I'm supposed to go every week for a while. I just wanted you to know."

"Good. I'm glad you're going to see him."

"Well, that's all I wanted to say." He gets up and walks back in his office.

I'm glad he's going to get some help. When we were first dating, he mentioned once that he felt depressed, and then a few weeks later he was fine. I knew nothing about depression and had no idea it was going to be a life-long problem for him. I didn't know there was anything like chronic depression. I'm sure he didn't either. He works hard controlling his anger, which goes hand in hand with depression, but he retreats to his room and his computer and withdraws from all of us too often. I wish that I were more exciting or pleasing to be with. I tried for years to think of fun things for us to do. But the truth was, I had very little to do with the problem.

I worry about Don. He never says much, but now he works and helps out, then retreats into a world that I can't reach. I just wish that we could share our lives. But what is there to share but sadness and frustration? I can't lift his spirits; he can't do anything for mine. We retreat to our separate worlds, and I hope we'll still be together when this is all over.

I'm very tired, and walk past his office on the way to bed. He's busy typing something on the computer. One light pools by his screen. The rest of the room is so dark.

"Good night, hon." I say as I pass by.

"Oh, good night."

March 5, 1987

We're in the middle of a very long Mass, and the chords of "Praise to the Lord, the Almighty, the King of Creation" fade away. The words stick in my mind as the priest drones on. I start thinking about why Laura was punished by God. It would make more sense if I had been punished.

But where was her sin? She's an innocent five-year old. Where was her evil, to deserve such a fate? Her face scarred, her leg and arm paralyzed, her eye sightless forever.

I'm grateful she's alive, and for her amazing recovery. But I can't accept His cruelty to her, to all the children who suffer needlessly. The ones paralyzed and sightless and mindless, who suffer for sins never committed. I still mouth the words to "Praise to the Lord, the King of Creation," but inside I hate Him.

In spite of these despairing thoughts, I enroll David in a religion class at church. He tells me that he raised his hand when the teacher asked if there were any atheists or agnostics in the class.

Just because I've lost my faith, doesn't mean I wish that for my children. I just want them to be happy. I'm so close to being an atheist myself. And my growing lack of belief has brought me no joy, only a loss.

Despite my doubts, I think believing can make people better. Believing can give so much joy. Believing in God gives meaning to the universe and a purpose to life. Believing helps us focus on the really important things in life, like love and the equality of all people.

So if I think believing is so great, then why am I having such a difficult time with it? My difficulty is not with Christian morality or the church. My problem is with God. The universe is too random, evolution so full of chance, that I just can't believe there is a hidden being in charge of everything. When I find a quote by Carl Sagan, "Extraordinary claims require extraordinary evidence," it makes so much sense. There will never be any proof of God, but there should be some sort of evidence. And there isn't any.

Other times, I think about the miracles of Lourdes, which I still hang onto as my childhood blanket, hoping they might be true. There are so many coincidences and dreams bordering on the psychic and so much that can't be explained, and God seems a perfectly good answer. Or rather, He used to be a good answer. I certainly would be happier and more joyful if there were a God. I don't want to die and suddenly cease to exist. I need to keep searching for meaning. I can't stop looking for God, hoping to believe in Him or Her someday.

Still, I wonder why I am so compelled to keep on this mad treasure hunt. Maybe it's time to throw away the old tattered childhood security blanket. But it's so hard. Without it, there is nothing to hold onto, just emptiness.

April 11, 1987

We will need an expert witness for the lawsuit, and we also want to test Laura's cognitive skills before she goes to a regular school. Rich chooses Dr. Paul Satz, head of the Neuropsychiatric Institute at UCLA, for Laura's psychological testing. Even if we don't need the report for the lawsuit, we need it for her future.

Laura and I drive up to Los Angeles, another early morning rush hour drive, but at least it's not for an operation. I tell her it's going to be fun. People will be asking her lots of questions. That's all. Nothing scary.

Dr. Satz interviews Laura for the entire morning, while I sit in the psychiatric waiting room. I try to read, but after a few minutes I give up and watch the people. This isn't Orange County with its plush waiting rooms and Newport Beach blondes. This is the middle of Los Angeles, and poor and uninsured people from all over the city come to this clinic. A homeless woman, with bags and all her belongings in a grocery cart, waits in the lobby, swaying back and forth. One man argues loudly with no one. There's no difference between white, black and Hispanic in this waiting room. Finally, close to noon, Laura comes to the door with Dr. Satz, and stares at a man in rags who is waving his hand frantically. We walk to a Burger King in the next block.

"Why can't anyone help that man?"

"They're trying to help him, honey, but sometimes it takes a long time."

Laura describes all the tests to me. She really liked the one where she drew her family. I ask her what she drew. Her answer will show a lot about how she sees her place in the family. I've read about similar tests.

"Well, I drew you and Dad and David and Sylbuster and Star."

"Where were you in the picture?" That would probably show her feeling of self worth.

"I didn't draw myself."

"You didn't? Why not?" I wonder if Laura might have more issues about self-image than I thought.

"Well, I was the one drawing the picture. Why would I put myself in it if I was drawing it?"

I laugh. Let them evaluate that.

May 1987

Don and I receive a phone call one evening from Richard de Chambeau, a lobbyist and wildlife specialist in Sacramento.

"I'd like to talk to you about the mountain lion moratorium." I call Don to the phone so we can all talk together.

"The moratorium is a really hot issue in Sacramento right now, because the Department of Fish and Game will be voting soon on its continuation."

Don and I know that much, but not much more. Richard tells us about how the mountain lion has been protected for the last 15 years, even though it has never been endangered.

"There are over five thousand mountain lions in California. They come on ranches, killing livestock, and attack horses. They're completely fearless. They have no natural predators, so they drink from swimming pools in people's backyards and kill their pets. There are a lot of people who believe we need some limited hunting of the mountain lion, but the opposition is great."

Don and I haven't gotten into the politics of the mountain lion issue. We've been too busy with Laura, and I can see both sides of the issue. I don't want the animal hunted and killed. I don't think anyone has the right to kill another living creature.

On the other hand, if the mountain lion has no predators, its numbers will increase and there will be more attacks. Richard and Don and I talk for a long time. He wants us to make a statement before the legislature votes. The only reason we agree is because we don't want another attack. We want the moratorium to end and for there to be controlled hunting, but only because of the danger to people.

We fly up to Sacramento. I'm not a good speaker, but Don really doesn't want to read our statement, so I do.

We walk in a large assembly hall filled with legislators and reporters and I'm led up on stage to the podium. I look out into a sea of hostile and indifferent faces. I feel stupid. I remind myself I'm an intelligent woman with a master's degree. I want to convince and persuade these people. I want to impress them. But it's all I can do to stumble through the written statement without too many mistakes, and then it's over. I feel myself shrinking at the podium. My confidence plummets.

Everyone in that hall has already taken sides. And the sides are clearly drawn. Nobody's going to switch opinions because some mother tells about her daughter's attack. One side wants to preserve the mountain lion. Some mountain lion advocates love the animal more than they love humans, and blame the people who are crowding the mountain lion out of its territory. There's even a group called 'Earth First' that has threatened to blow up the Department of Fish and Game if they don't extend the moratorium. The other side, ranchers, hunters, and the NRA, wants the moratorium to end, and wants controlled hunting of the lion.

If it weren't for Laura, I'd be on the side protecting the mountain lion. But seeing my daughter in the mouth of a mountain lion changed my opinion. I don't want anyone else to go through that.

We fly back home that evening. Laura and David are at a friends for the night. Don heads off to bed, and as I flick on the kitchen light, I notice little green bugs everywhere. It takes me a few minutes to remember our praying mantis egg case. We kept it on the kitchen counter all winter, and wondered when they were going to hatch. I didn't think it would be tonight.

I call Don before he gets in bed, and we tear off little pieces of newspaper and gather up praying mantis babies. They we hurry outside and gently set them in the bushes and flowerbeds. There must be hundreds; I lose track of the times we run outside with two or three on a piece of paper.

Finally we look around the kitchen. I don't see anything crawling. It's almost midnight. We sit down at the kitchen table, exhausted.

Don looks at me. "It's a little ironic that we spend the day in Sacramento trying to get mountain lions killed, and we come home and spend two hours trying to save praying mantis babies. Is there something wrong with this picture?"

I start laughing, and we have the best laugh we've had in months.

The committee votes to allow hunting, which is exactly what we wanted, but then the legal battle begins. The moratorium is over on paper, but not in reality.

June 10, 1987

David finishes fourth grade next week. He's had a terrible school year. He wasn't motivated and his teacher didn't communicate with us. And yet we know that David is very smart. He loves learning about things he's interested in.

My brother-in-law, Ed Harper, was one of the original members of the Black Sheep Squadron in World War Two, and is now a Vice-President of McDonnell Douglas in St. Louis. He took us on a tour of the facility last year, and fueled David's love of airplanes. David knows every fighter jet in every Air Force in the world. One evening at dinner, I asked him how many countries he could name, and he not only named over one hundred countries, he described their aircraft in detail.

He loves skateboarding and bikes and baseball, and he remembers everything he reads.

Now his science teacher calls to tell me that David scored higher than any other student on his state-wide science test.

"Wow, that's wonderful."

"There's something else…"

More? I'm so proud of David already.

"He's flunking science and he really needs to get his grade up to a D before I can give him the science award."

"How could he be flunking? You said he scored the highest on the test!"

"Because he hasn't handed in any homework in the last two months. Haven't you been getting the notices?"

After school that day, Dave and I have a long talk. He assures me that he will finish the homework, and gives me the old line about how horrible the science teacher is and how everybody hates her.

After Dave goes to his room to do his homework, I walk outside for a while and sit in the garden. David's doing badly, and a lot of it is my fault. I just don't have the time. Ninety percent of my time is spent on Laura, and I don't see any other way it can be. Now, in addition to feeling guilty about not saving Laura, I'm neglecting David, losing my faith, and not communicating with Don. The list is overwhelming. I wish I could just sit here in my garden and stare at the plants and trees forever.

Chapter 17

June, 1987

Laura's school requests a meeting, so one afternoon Don and I drive down to R.H. Dana. Laura's busy at therapy while we sit in an empty classroom with the principal, her first grade teacher, and special education teacher.

"Would you like some coffee?" the principal asks. He's around fifty, impeccably dressed, and it seems like he runs the school as well as he dresses.

Don accepts a cup, but I just fold my hands on my lap. I'm eyeing a plate of store-bought sugar cookies in the center of the table, wondering if I should reach for one. I resist.

"We called this meeting because we think Laura is ready to be transferred into a regular classroom at your home school, Olivewood Elementary."

I'm glad I don't have a cup of hot coffee. I would have spilled it.

No. Absolutely not. Impossible. She's not ready. I don't say the words, but they're on my tongue, ready.

"We've talked about it at length, and the whole team has decided it's the best thing for Laura."

Don says, "I think that's a good idea." I glance at him. Traitor.

As politely as I can, I ask, "What about her therapy?"

"There's another school much closer to you where she can have therapy two or three times a week, so that shouldn't be a problem."

Don nods his head, and I can't think of an argument fast enough. Just like that, the principal is thanking everyone and the meeting is over. I'm convinced Laura's not ready for a regular classroom, but everyone else thinks she is.

We walk to the therapy room to get Laura, who walks slowly to greet us. Her helmet covers her head, her sightless eye looks red and raw, and her scars are still visible. She walks with a noticeable limp.

The ride home is silent. Don drives, oblivious to my frustration. I don't want to talk about this with Laura in the car, so I wait till later in the evening, when we're alone in front of the TV.

"Don? We need to talk about this school thing."

"Ok, what about it?"

"She's not ready. She has the expanders in her scalp; she's still wearing the helmet. She's just not ready for a regular classroom. Can you imagine how the kids will treat her?"

"She's going to be fine. And she won't have that long bus ride every day."

"I know she's not ready, and neither am I." I don't know what other argument will work.

"It's not good for her to be with the special kids either. She's not learning very much. And she's in a regular first grade classroom for a few hours every day, anyway."

I argue with myself for days, but a few days later I sit out on the curb with Laura, waiting for the bus. After it picks her up, I go inside and clean up, do the dishes, go outside and work in the garden. I look at my watch. It's been an hour and she's still on the bus. The ride is only a half hour, but picking up other students turns it into an hour each way. That's two hours a day harnessed into a bus seat with nothing to do. Almost anything would be better than that.

Laura accepts the decision with a shrug. She likes the idea of going to David's school. I feel a little better knowing he'll be there with her. Actually, he's in a different classroom and on a different schedule, so they'll never see each other. But Olivewood is only a few blocks from home, so by the end of the summer, I've gotten myself used to the idea. I grudgingly accept that it's the right decision. I hope so.

September 12, 1987

David has a classmate named Andrew. His mom asks if I can watch her daughter after school. I agree. Emily is only a year older than Laura and they can play together. I pick up Emily and Laura from school, and we get in the car.

"When we get home, you and Laura can play with her new ponies, or maybe watch a movie."

Emily turns to Laura and says, "I don't play with people who look like you." I can see her clearly in the rear view mirror. She makes a sour face and sticks out her tongue at Laura.

I've heard the expression "seeing red" but I never knew what it meant before. I clench the steering wheel.

I try to control my voice. "That's not very nice."

Emily crosses her skinny arms in front of her, "I'm not going to play with HER."

Laura is silent and looks out the other window without a change of expression. I want to pull over and tell Emily to get out of the car, but of course I can't do that. I have to put up with this girl and protect Laura for the next three hours.

I'm glad it's a short ride home, because my hands are clenched tight and my stomach is churning. I help Laura out of the car and we walk inside. I have to decide what to do with Emily. I don't want her in my house. I say roughly, "You just sit here and watch a movie, Emily. Laura and I are going outside to play."

I plant Emily in front of the TV with an old Strawberry Shortcake movie that Laura has seen a thousand times and go outside with Laura. I bring a chocolate snack out for us. I can't even ask Emily if she wants one. I'm furious. I don't want her to have any fun. I hate what she's done to Laura. Laura and I laugh and play outside. I look in at Emily through the sliding glass door. She sits zombie-like in front of the TV, just a few feet away. I don't care. I relish the thought of not caring.

I can't bring myself to speak to her, and I won't let Laura near her. David comes in from skateboarding and out to the back yard. I grab him.

"Dave, could you please play with Laura till that girl goes home? I'll explain later. I'll be back out in a minute."

"Sure, ok," David says and runs over to Laura. I sit in the kitchen staring at Emily in the living room, a tiny girl who is too young for me to hate. But I can't get rid of my anger. I go back outside and position myself where I can keep an eye on Emily through the sliding glass door, and count the minutes till her mother comes back.

Finally I hear the doorbell. I grab Emily not so gently and propel her to the front door with her stupid Disney backpack.

"How was everything?" Her mom smiles.

I tell her what Emily said, just barely able to get the words out.

She laughs. "Oh, I'm sorry. Kids are so mean sometimes." She glances at Emily, but doesn't say anything and gives her a kiss. "Come on, sweetie, let's go."

They walk hand in hand down the concrete sidewalk. Emily laughs and bounces next to her mom. I know right then that Emily's mom won't say anything to her. I can see Emily the adult, perhaps beautiful on the outside, but sour and nasty to the core, like those hard candies that taste bitter to the very end.

Laura and David are playing. As I watch them, my anger slowly slips away. I go outside and give Laura and David a big bear hug that surprises them. I want to give them the world for being so wonderful, but I feel useless. I couldn't protect Laura from the mountain lion or the suffering that came after. And now, I can't even protect her from a nasty seven-year old.

The intensity of my anger surprises me. Emily isn't responsible for what she says. But when I think about it, I get furious all over again.

I begin to watch people more carefully, trying to protect Laura from everyone who might hurt her. But I know I can't, and that hurts more than anything.

October 13, 1987

I decide to sing in the choir again. Linda's found a new accompanist; I don't have the time or desire to play for them. I just want to be part of the group. Linda asks me one evening to play a line on the synthesizer, along with the organist. I start to play a few notes, but suddenly I can't breathe. I get up quickly and walk outside. I realize that I'm terrified of playing. I drive home without even going back in the church.

I can't play in front of people anymore. I've gotten more and more nervous for months, but didn't realize how bad it was until now. I've played the piano my whole life, and have performed for large groups since I was in elementary school. I've always had the usual butterflies before performances, but I've never been <u>afraid</u> to play. I've always been proud that I could come into a concert as a last minute substitute, and play beautifully with no practice. I've played for shows, Christmas concerts, made CD's in recording studios, and suddenly I can't play one simple line in front of a church choir?

When David asks about our annual Christmas party, I put off answering him, saying we might not have time this year. I can't even tell my family that I'm scared to play a few Christmas carols in front of friends.

One day I talk to my friend Kathy. She's in the choir and saw what happened a few weeks earlier. I tell her how frightened I am and that I don't understand what's happening.

"Well, of course, that makes sense."

"What do you mean?"

"You've been through this horrible trauma. You're trying to put your life back together. You're doing a great job with yourself and your family and Laura's health and the lawsuit, so something has to fall apart. You should be glad it's the piano. It'll come back when things get better."

I think about what she says and it feels right. I'm holding together a balloon that's bulging out on all sides, ready to burst. Maybe the piano is the least important thing right now.

Even knowing what might be the cause, there's nothing I can do to make my fear go away. I stay away from choir. I keep practicing alone and hope my friend is right.

Chapter 18

October 26, 1987

Don is included in the lawsuit, but the county files a motion to get him dismissed since he didn't actually see the lion. A new state law says that you have to actually witness an accident, or you can't collect any damages. The fact that Laura is Don's child, that he saw her minutes after the attack, and that the incident affected his whole life, doesn't matter. The motion might go all the way to the Supreme Court of California.

Then the county files another unexpected motion to get the whole case dismissed.

"They can do this?" I ask Mike.

"Oh, yeah, they do it all the time. Don't worry, it doesn't mean anything. They're not going to get the case dismissed."

The morning of the court hearing comes. Alone at home, I go out to the garden and pretend that everyone connected with the county is a weed, and finish weeding most of the garden. I wipe the dirt off my watch. The motion should have been heard by now.

The phone rings and I run back inside, catching my breath.

It's Rich calling from the courthouse. He doesn't sound happy. "We lost the motion."

"What's next? We can do something, can't we? I mean, this isn't the end of the lawsuit, is it?"

"No, no. I'll file an appeal but that might take months. Don't worry. We just have to get in front of another judge and they might give a completely different ruling. Don't worry. I've got to go. My plane is boarding."

I hang up the phone and call Don, who's too busy at work to say much. I can tell he's upset. I call Mike, who's still optimistic. "It's only one ruling. We can appeal it and win. We have a great case."

"Yeah, I know, but if we can't even get to trial, it won't be worth anything to have a great case."

"No, I'm serious. Don't think that way. These things happen all the time. You just go back and try again in front of a different judge."

October 30

I'm opening a can of cat food when Rich calls back, a few days later.

After we say hello, he hesitates for a second.

"Hey, you know, the day I left Orange County after the hearing? Well, this is pretty funny. I ran like crazy out to the plane, jumped up the steps and found my seat. Everything's good. We're taxiing down the runway and the flight attendant says, 'Welcome to flight 84 to Newark, New Jersey.' I was so upset about the motion that I got on the wrong plane."

I laugh. Poor Rich. That was a long flight to New Jersey and back to San Jose, California. What a story. But as I'm wondering why he's telling me this, he says,

"Anyway, I had a long time to think, Sue, and I've decided to give your case to another lawyer. There's just too much publicity and I've never had a case go to the Supreme Court. I just think someone else would do a better job."

I sit down at the table with the open cat food can in my hand, unable to speak. This is the end of our case. Our lawyer doesn't even want it.

"Hey, Sue, are you still there? Don't be upset. I already found someone. I think you're going to like the new guy. His name is Wylie Aitken and he's down in Santa Ana, real close to you guys. It'll be a lot easier for him since he's already in Orange County."

I can hardly listen. I feel abandoned. He's just giving the case to another lawyer. We've lost the case. Just because this lawyer is close by doesn't mean he's any good. He's just taking a discarded case that even Rich doesn't want. I'm not encouraged. We talk for a few more minutes and then hang up.

After dinner, Don and I sit at the table and talk.

Don isn't as upset as I am. "Well, we knew it was coming," he reminds me. "He's never taken a case to the Supreme Court and I know he was worried."

"His trip to New Jersey gave him too much time to think. I wish he had gotten on the right plane."

"Maybe it's a good thing. Rich really doesn't have that much experience. I think he was in way over his head. Plus, he hated all the publicity. Maybe the new lawyer is good, too."

I still feel abandoned and chase a few peas around the plate with my fork. "If the new lawyer is so good, why didn't he take the case in the beginning? He knew about it. It was all over the papers. No one besides Rich ever thought we had a chance against the county. Actually, that was Mike."

Don shrugs. "Yeah, well, I guess we'll meet the new lawyer and see what he's like."

Don heads off to the computer; neither one of us feels like talking. I walk to the back yard, take the broom and start sweeping the patio. With each sweep, I think of a new word. Anger. Frustration. Abandonment. Sadness. Fear. Hopelessness. This is ridiculous. I have to do something. I put down the broom, go back inside and call my friend Rhonda, the one who set up the trust fund. Her husband Jim answers. He's a corporate lawyer, but I'm hoping he's at least heard of Aitken.

"Have you ever heard of Wylie Aitken?" I don't feel like wasting words.

"Yeah, I have."

I don't want to tell Jim that Wylie's taking over our case, because that might influence what he says. "Give me a one-line summary of what you know about him."

"Hmmm. One line? Ok. He's a hard hitter, deals only with seven digits, and has never lost a case."

"Thanks, that's all I need to know."

Jim laughs. "Well now, tell me what's going on."

"He's coming in to take our case."

"That's good, Sue, it really is. He has a great reputation. He's one of the best."

After I hang up I feel much better, although I want to meet this Wylie as soon as possible. I want to know if we still have a chance.

October 1987

The sky is grey with early morning fog, and I'm sitting at the kitchen table with a steaming cup of hot chocolate. Don is at work, David and Laura have gone to school, and I'm by myself.

I stare into the cup and realize I have nowhere to go and nothing to do all day. Oh, I have shopping and cleaning, and chores and laundry. Laura has a blood test this afternoon at Mission, a doctor's appointment tomorrow, and therapy three afternoons a week. I have things to do. Just not right this minute.

I feel empty inside. Other people's lives are going somewhere; I'm just catching up to where we were before Laura got hurt.

I know I'm whining and complaining, and I shouldn't. Laura is alive, and I want to take care of her and help her. This is my job as her mother. But nobody seems to care anymore. I wish I could have put some of that love and support in a bank, and could start taking it out now. I love my family, but I want a life too. I want to go somewhere. I want to do something important, something significant.

Years ago, in an American literature class, I read, "Most men lead lives of quiet desperation." I knew that would never be me. I had great plans for the future. I was going to do amazing things for the world. How wrong I was.

I finish my drink and get up slowly. I have lots of things to do before the day is over.

October 1987

"Sue, hurry up. We don't want to be late," Don calls from the living room. I throw on a red blouse and black slacks, then run outside, where Don's waiting in the car.

I hope we like Mr. Wylie Aitken, and, more importantly, I hope he's good. His office is on the eighth floor of a sleek high rise, right across from the Orange County Courthouse in Santa Ana. We take the garage elevators to the main floor, where an elevator attendant asks whom we're visiting.

"Wylie Aitken." The attendant smiles broadly like we got the right answer on a game show and escorts us onto the elevator.

When the door opens, the first thing I see is marble floors and elegant furniture. I look down the hallway for Wylie's office. Then I realize that this entire floor is his office. Don and I walk to an ornate wooden desk where a secretary politely asks our names. Beyond her, I can see into a law library. The Oriental carpet is thick under my black heels. The secretary invites us to sit down and offers drinks. We both ask for Cokes.

When a slight man strides into the reception area, Don and I both stand.

"Hi, I'm Wylie," he says smiling, and shakes my hand with a perfect grip. His hair is silver but he looks young and fit. His smile is contagious but his voice is like gravel. I wonder how people can listen to him in the courtroom. He leads us to his office, where we sit in green leather library chairs from a century past. Two walls are filled with law books, and the other two are floor to ceiling windows looking far out to the ocean over a wintery Orange County.

As Wylie sits at his desk, I see a large portrait of Robert Kennedy behind him. I loved Robert Kennedy. I'm ridiculously relieved: Wylie must be a Democrat. There aren't many Democrats in Orange County. It's like finding the perfect chocolate in a box of See's candy. I like him instantly.

Wylie does most of the talking, and while he does, he removes his small wire-rimmed glasses and puts them back on constantly. He's talking about the county's immunities and about the last motion that we lost. He wants to file a motion to get the case back on track. What's more important, he seems confident that we'll win.

Wyllie tells us that he wants to record our recollections of the day of the attack. I'm the first to talk. I've gotten so tired of telling the story over and over. I use the same words, the same inflections, almost like it's memorized, but this time I get caught up in the story again. I feel myself back there, looking at the matted fur of the mountain lion as it holds Laura by the neck. I can see the drops of blood splatter onto the sandy soil. I can feel my mind go blank as Greg pushes his way past me.

The room is quiet when I finish. Wylie clicks off the tape recorder, but doesn't say anything. It's time for Don's story. I can't listen. It was hard enough for me to tell the story again. I look around the room and notice a thirteen-starred American flag, tattered and torn, displayed in a glass case on the wall.

Don is finished. I pay attention again.

Wylie looks at him over the top of his wire-rimmed glasses with a pleasant smile. "Don, did you actually see the lion?"

For a second I hope Don will say he saw the lion. If only he did, it would mean he could get part of the settlement, the money he deserves. He went through as much sorrow and suffering as I did. I'd back up whatever he says.

But of course Don will never lie-I know that well. He won't lie even when I want him to, those white lies about liking a dress, or a birthday present, or if I've lost weight. Sometimes I wish that he would lie just to be polite, but he never does.

"No, I didn't see the lion."

"Well, you know it'll be difficult to keep you as part of the lawsuit. The county will use this new law to keep you from claiming any injuries. A law just down from the Supreme Court..."

"Oh yeah," I interrupt without thinking. "Rich told us about that woman whose son was run over in front of the house and she ran out seconds after the accident, but couldn't collect damages."

"Yes, that's it," replies Wylie. "The law now says you have to be there contemporaneously—at the same time as the accident. You have to see it happen."

He talks to us for a while about how difficult it is to sue the county and all the pitfalls that will occur in the future of the lawsuit. He exudes confidence and he's completely professional. Rich was friendly and easy to talk to, but what good did that do?

Wylie dismisses us when he's finished, and says he'll keep us informed on the Supreme Court documents. He wants to meet Laura, and I promise to bring her in soon.

We shake hands, and walk down the corridor. As we wait silently for the elevator, I think of the large portrait of Robert Kennedy. I decide it's a good sign. Maybe we can win after all.

November 5, 1987

Laura and I are sitting at the kitchen table. She's doing homework and I'm writing invoices for Don's business.

Laura looks up. "I have to write an answer to this question. 'What is the most important thing that's happened to you in the past two years?'"

My mind is a kaleidoscope of swirling colors and events. How can she possibly answer that? The attack, the operations, the lawsuit, her grandpa, the aplastic anemia. There's so much.

"So what are you going to put down?"

"I already got it done. I wrote, 'I got an allowance and we got a new cat.'" She pushes the paper off to the side and smiles her lopsided smile.

She's gone on to her math homework, but I sit there thinking about the last two years. Laura's answer is not what I expected. It was just an ordinary answer to a simple question. And her life this past year has been anything but ordinary.

I always wanted an amazing life-to see marvelous places and do great things. Be the amazing person who won awards and changed the world.

Now I sit in my ordinary house, with a good family and two cats, and I'm happy. I have the ability to speak, walk, and see. I have enough food and I have a home. Maybe Laura is right. It's wonderful to be ordinary.

November 21, 1987

I bring Laura to meet Wylie on a Thursday afternoon. Laura is polite and a little shy with Wylie, but they go into his office and talk for a while. Wylie takes me aside while Laura is entertained by his secretary.

"She's very articulate and bright. She'll be great on the witness stand." He seems pleased and talks about the new motion.

As I listen to Wylie, I can't help but compare him to Rich. Rich seemed like a good lawyer, but I realize now that he was in over his head. We became friends with him, which I thought was good, but it made it harder to be abandoned by him.

Wylie is brilliant. He loves publicity, which is perfect for our case. Plus, I hear that he's incredible in the courtroom.

All the investigative work has been done. The case is ready for Wylie to win or lose. Someone tells me he's in the "100 Best Lawyers in America." I look it up in the library one afternoon and it's true. I just hope he's good enough to win our case.

Chapter 19

Laura with friend Theresa

Credit: Los Angeles Times

December 1, 1987

Laura has very few friends, probably because she looks so different. The scars on her face are healing well, but are still obvious. She wears a brace and she limps. Her right eye looks terrible and most difficult of all is that she still has to wear the bicycle helmet all the time. I can understand how children might not want to play with her. I wish I could make them see how much fun she is, but I can't make friends for her.

Don and I decide that we all need a vacation. We might not be able to do much about the lawsuit or Laura's skills in the classroom, but we can try to have some fun. We've never been to Hawaii, and decide to go for ten days at Christmas, just the four of us.

December 20

Don and I are standing waist deep in the ocean at Olawalu on Maui. Laura tiptoes, just barely touching the bottom, with mask and snorkel, and puts her head in the water for the first time. She screams in delight, pops up and pulls the mask off. "There's fish. I saw a red and yellow one!" I help her put the mask back on. She yells in delight and pops up again, excited.

"Try to keep your head down and look at them." I tell her.

"Ok."

We hold her as we walk out into slightly deeper water. David is already about twenty feet away, oblivious to the rest of us. Laura puts her face in again. This time it's only a second before she's up, pulling off the mask. "Did you see that? That one with the brown spots?"

I finally put on my mask and go under with her. Her hands are pointing everywhere, first one fish, then another, and another. She manages to keep her face down for a few minutes, getting used to the snorkel, then she can't stand being silent, and pulls her head out of the water and yells.

We're all laughing so much we hate to get out of the water. Every day we swim in the ocean, and visit the beautiful sights on the island. It's hard to go back to Orange County.

Laura's blood count goes up at her next test, a good sign. I wonder if it was the fruit juice, the pomegranate, orange and guava drink that we loved in Hawaii. I start giving her lots of vitamin C, just in case.

March 15, 1988

Whether it was the vacation or the vitamins, Laura's blood count is high enough by spring to put the plate in her skull. Dr. Watanabe carefully explains everything at our next visit.

"Laura, I'm going to put two balloons called expanders under your scalp. See this long tube? It will come out behind your ear and I'll fill the expanders with a saline solution— that's just salt water. We're going to stretch the skin on your head so it will cover the plate."

"Why can't you just use the skin that's over the area now?" I ask.

"The skin that was transplanted from her leg has no blood supply of its own. It gets its blood supply from the tissue under it. But when we put the plastic plate in, the skin won't have any blood supply. That's why we have to use the actual skin from her scalp."

"How long will it take?"

"Well, it's March now. The problem is that Laura's skin is so scarred that it's very difficult to stretch. If we can use two expanders, maybe June or July. If we need another expander, it'll take longer."

Don and I decide to go ahead with the operation. It's essential that Dr. Palmer can put in the plate that will cover the exposed area of brain. Plus, Laura will look more like the other children when it's over. Hopefully she will be free from the meanness and rudeness of her classmates and strangers. I wonder if it might already be too late. Laura, who used to be so outgoing, now approaches other people cautiously. She has an " I won't like you, so you can't hurt me" attitude toward others. It hurts to see this in her at such a young age.

Laura's blood count is high. If it goes down again, it might be years before she has another chance.

After the operation, Laura's head doesn't look any worse. The expanders are barely noticeable. Twice a week Dr. Watanabe injects more liquid, as much as Laura can stand without crying. I hold her hand. It's torture to watch, but we have no other choice. We have to get the plate in to protect her head. The area where the skull is missing is only covered by the dura, the thick skin-like substance covering the brain itself. I can see the brain pulsate with each heartbeat. I worry more and more about injuries to her head. It was bad enough with the soft area, but now she has bags over her head that might break at any time. Her helmet starts getting tight. We buy another larger helmet, hoping it will be the last one.

Every time I wash her hair, I cringe when I feel the soft watery expanders with the thin flesh covering them. I can't put any pressure on them. I'm so afraid the skin will tear. Tears come to my eyes when I think of all she's been through. But maybe this will be the last insult. I can only hope.

September 1988

At the end of September, Laura has the third expander put in, and Dr. Watanabe starts the horrible process of filling the new one while continuing to expand the old ones. Looking at her poor head, I'm convinced there has to be enough skin, but Dr. Watanabe has to be absolutely sure. There are no second chances with this operation.

We have an appointment with Dr. Watanabe two days before the surgery. I've noticed a red area on one of the expanders, and my heart practically stops when he says, "Yes, the skin is starting to tear. We'll have to take some liquid out. And it looks like there's an infection starting. We'll put her on antibiotics."

Even if there's not enough skin, we have to go ahead with the next surgery because Laura's skin can't stretch anymore. I'm dreading this operation. There are so many things that could go wrong.

The surgeons have to drill into her skull to attach the lexan plate that will cover the exposed area. I don't even ask Dr. Palmer to explain the surgery. I really don't want to know. Once they have the plate in place, they'll pull the scalp over the area and hope there's enough skin to cover it.

Dr. Palmer and Dr. Watanabe meet with Don and me before surgery. They're planning to cut Laura's hair just at the site of the surgery. They assure her they won't cut off the hair she's been growing back for two years.

Don and I sit in the waiting room, the same one we were in for the first operation. I can't help but remember the horror of that first night. I don't even try to read a magazine, but just stare at the wall. After three hours Dr. Palmer walks into the waiting room, pulling off his surgical mask.

"Laura's fine, but I'm sorry, we had to shave her head." He looks at us sadly.

I sigh with relief when I hear the operation went well. Who cares about her hair? Dr. Palmer tells us he gave her a blood transfusion, which Don and I aren't happy about, but it's too late to do anything. Dr. Cairo had told us that in case of a bone marrow transplant, which seems less and less likely, a blood transfusion decreases the chance of success. But Laura had lots of blood transfusions when she was first attacked, so it probably doesn't matter.

Dr. Palmer continues. "We left some hair at the back of her head. We didn't know whether to shave it off or leave it. So we decided to leave it. We're not very good barbers." He shrugs his shoulders. I feel like laughing. I don't care whether they're "good barbers." "Good surgeons" is way more important.

Dr. Watanabe comes in and apologizes about her hair. This focus on a seemingly minor detail shows how much they care about Laura as a person.

Don and I walk through the double doors to the recovery room, put on the familiar green booties and mask, and go in to see Laura. She looks better than I expected, probably because of the transfusion. Her head is all bandaged. I can't tell if the red stains are Benadryl or blood. She's beginning to wake up, so I hand her the pink bunny we brought from home, and we talk for a few minutes.

I expected that with the horrible six-month preparation time for this operation, that the operation and recovery would be just as difficult.

But the next morning Dr. Palmer breezes into the hospital room.

"Hi, Laura, how are you feeling?"

Laura smiles. "Fine."

"Well, how would you like to go home today?"

"Today?" That's impossible. I stop, my hand in mid-air, reaching to open the blinds.

"Sure. She looks great. I'll check with Dr. Watanabe and we'll sign the discharge papers."

He's out the door, and I run to the phone to call Don.

"Laura's coming home today! Can you come down here and help us?"

"Today?" Don needs a moment to regroup, but says he'll be down as quickly as he can.

I find Laura's clothes and help her get dressed. We're both elated that she'll be out in a few hours, instead of days. I grab stuffed animals and cards and books and my suitcase and run out to the car.

"Mom, could I be a doctor for Halloween? We could take some of the blue shoe covers and a mask and I could be a surgeon."

"I don't think you'll be going anywhere for Halloween."

Don walks in and we leave the hospital in record time. The last operation is over and Laura will never have to wear a helmet again.

Later that evening I walk with Laura over to Kelli's next door to get a few pieces of candy-then it's back home to rest. But David has everything planned.

"Mom, I'll take two big garbage bags and tell everyone my sister was in the hospital and couldn't come."

"Sure, Dave." I can't help smiling. "I wouldn't believe it if some kid came to my door and told me that just to get some extra candy."

"But it's true."

"I know it's true, and you know its true, but that doesn't mean anybody's going to believe you. And I don't think you need the huge garbage bags!"

"I think you're wrong." He heads out the door with his two skateboarder friends.

Two hours later the door opens and David throws two bulging bags filled with candy on the living room floor. Laura squeals with excitement. She gives David a big hug and they start to go through their yearly ritual of sorting candy.

I stare at the bags.

"I don't believe it."

"There was only one person who kind of laughed and didn't give me an extra set. Only one person."

So Laura has her Halloween, thanks to her brother.

Chapter 20

Sledding in St. Louis

December 1988

The kids and I go to St. Louis for Christmas. Don has to work. David and Laura pray hard for snow, and, a few days later, it snows seven inches.

But even a simple prayer for snow gets me arguing with myself about God. Maybe God did hear those prayers, but I really doubt it. What about all the people who didn't want snow, and the people who will be killed and injured on the highways because of it? Why do I have to turn snow into a theological argument? I guess until I find an answer. I hope it's soon, because even I'm tired of my own incessant questioning every minute of every day.

Our St. Louis relatives aren't happy, but the three of us from California are ecstatic about the snow. We go to Target and buy sleds, those big red round ones. We try the park behind my parent's apartment and the little slopes are perfect for Laura, but David sees a picture of Art Hill, in front of the St. Louis Art Museum. Some kids had sledded right into the lake at the bottom. I'll drive over there to show them. It's just ten minutes away.

David pleads with me to take the sleds, just in case.

"Ok, put the sleds in the trunk. Just in case. But don't count on it."

I know one thing—Laura isn't going down that hill, especially if she's going to end up in the lake. I'm not ready for that.

We stand at the top of Art Hill, our breath foggy in the crisp air, watching the people slide down the sheet of ice. The figures at the bottom look only an inch high. David doesn't say a word.

The lake is far from the end of the hill, and I don't see how anyone could slide into it unless they were trying.

"Well, go ahead, Dave."

He jumps on the red sled and goes skimming wildly down the hill. I hold my breath, but he slows and comes to a stop far from the lake. He's a small red dot at the bottom. Then he begins to trudge back up.

Laura stands next to me, looking like she would give anything to go and knowing that it's impossible. I haven't let her away from my side for three years. I would never let her do anything this dangerous.

David's out of breath and red-cheeked. "It was great, mom. Just once more, please, please, please."

Laura's voice slips in. "Mom, can I go with Dave? Please? Just once?"

I look at her and smile. "Yeah, go ahead."

She and David stare at me for a second before it sinks in.

"Yes!" she screams.

I give them the lecture, the one that no one listens to. Hold tight. Don't let go of David. Stop the sled in time. Be careful. Don't collide with anyone. And don't slide into the lake!

And then they're sliding quickly down the hill, Laura in front. I hold my breath as they weave between other sleds, faster. I lose them for a minute and then I see them again as they reach the bottom. They're so far away I can only guess that it's them. I hope it's them.

For a moment, my heart catches in my throat. Then I see David helping Laura climb the hill, slipping a few times, but not sliding all the way back down.

Laura's face is red and cold and shining when she reaches the top of the hill. David helps her back on the sled and they laugh as she falls right off the other side. Then he holds her tight and they push off again. I take a long cold breath and smile.

The kids go down the hill and trudge back up at least five more times, till they can barely stand. When I look at Laura's glowing face, their coats and fur hats and mittens covered with snow, and David rubbing his hands together and laughing, I know it was the right decision. It's time to get them home before they freeze.

Back at the tiny brick apartment, Mom fixes steaming cups of hot chocolate and cookies for the kids. They talk on and on about the ice on the hill, and the cold, and the snow. And the people and all the sleds, and how close they came to the lake. And Mom and Dad sit and listen and are impressed in all the right places, and Mom refills the hot chocolate and gets more cookies out of the cupboard.

As I sip my hot chocolate, my mom next to me, David and Laura red-cheeked and laughing, the world seems a much better place than I can remember in a long time. Who could have imagined, almost three years ago, that we'd arrive at this moment.

January, 1989

I'm in the middle of a convent dream, desperate to get everything packed so I can leave. Antiques, furniture; I didn't think I had so much to take with me. I have these dreams a lot. Suddenly I hear Don's voice. Why is he in the convent with me?

I open my eyes. He's standing next to the bed, still in his pajamas.

"The cars are gone. They're both gone!"

I blink and rub my eyes as I sit up. I don't know what he's talking about, but I don't think it's a dream.

"What?"

"Get up. We've been robbed!"

He's already running to Laura's room; I slip out from under the blankets and run to David's. We meet back in the bedroom. "Laura's fine. I woke her up."

"Dave's ok too."

We rush out to the family room. Don calls the police.

Dave walks sleepily out of his room. "What's wrong? What's the matter?"

I give him a hug. Don and the kids are fine. They're all that matters to me. I look around the living room. The TV and the VCR are gone; movies are scattered on the carpet. The microwave is gone. We look for anything else that might be missing.

The sliding glass door is slightly open. That's how they got in. By the time the police arrive, we realize that last night we had robbers in the house who managed to steal household items, carry them outside, find the keys to both cars, and drive away—without anyone waking up. I check the kids' rooms. Nothing seems to be missing. At least they didn't go in their bedrooms.

I sit down at the table, the breath forced out of me, spiraling down from euphoria about the kids being unharmed to a sudden panic at what could have happened.

The robbers had muddy shoes, because the detectives find shoe prints in front of the empty TV stand and by the front door. I notice fingerprints on the dusty videotapes on the floor.

"These must belong to the robbers. They're not ours."

A detective lifts a set of prints right off the top of the tapes.

The next morning we get a call from the police department. They ran the prints, found a name and address in San Diego, found both of our cars at a run-down apartment complex, and arrested the suspects.

When we get our Camry station wagon back, we find Carl's Jr. and McDonald's trash all over the back seat, soda cups and wadded up papers in the front, and a baby picture already taped to the dashboard. It just seems wrong to be a thief and have a baby. They certainly didn't waste anytime making themselves at home.

On the back seat, I see a pewter mug filled with coins. That's David's mug and was on his desk in his bedroom. I feel sick when I realize that David could have woken up.

Don and I talk about getting an alarm system or maybe a dog. Next time we might not be so lucky. Our luck seems to be measured not in how good things are, but how much worse they could have been. Does everyone live this way?

I don't know the answer. And even though life has gotten so much better than it was, bad luck seems to have become a way of life.

Chapter 21

Laura and Jim Abbott

June 1989

After Mike gave Dave a baseball bat and mitt, Dave fell in love with the game. He's on a Little League team, and we watch all the Angel games. The sports world is focused on Jim Abbott, the new pitcher for the Angels. The fact that he can't use his right hand and still manages to pitch for a major league team has impressed everyone. Laura's seen him on TV, and with

David's continuous commentary, he's really an inspiration to her.

David is out skateboarding with his friends one afternoon. Laura is sitting at the kitchen table, drawing. She loves to draw. I say, half joking, "You know, you could write a letter to Jim Abbott and tell him how much you admire him. People do that all the time. And wouldn't David be excited if Jim Abbott wrote back?"

"Could we, Mom? That would be really cool." She sits up straighter in the kitchen chair and wiggles with excitement. "But what would I say? I don't know how to write letters."

"Well, you could tell me what you want to say and I'll help you write it down."

"Let's do it. I can't wait till he writes back and David sees the letter."

Maybe I shouldn't have said anything. "Just because you write to him doesn't mean he'll write back. He probably gets thousands of letters. He won't have time to answer all of them. He might write back, but he might not."

She slumps down in her seat and plays with her hair.

"Well, let's do it anyway. We don't have anything to lose. It's the middle of June. If we don't hear back by the end of July, then he probably won't write back."

On Saturday, while David is out on the field, Laura and I sit in the bleachers and write the letter. She tells me what to say and I write it for her, then she prints her own words.

Mike stops by after the fourth inning.

Laura yells out, "Mike, look at this."

As he sits next to her, she pushes the letter into his hand. "Look what we're going to do. We're going to send this to Jim Abbott and then he's going to write back and David will be so excited!"

Mike reads the letter, "Hey, this is great. He will definitely write back."

Mike holds on to the letter. "Do you want me to get this to Jim Abbott?"

"Well sure, if you can."

"Of course I can." He sounds offended that I have such little faith in him.

"Thanks, and don't tell David that we wrote the letter. That's the big secret."

I figure Jim Abbot will get the letter, but we probably won't hear anything for a couple of weeks. I'm not counting on anything. Mike thinks that the whole world loves publicity, but it's not true.

Dave is off school on Friday. He sees the mailman walk across the front lawn.

"I'll get the mail," he calls.

He walks slowly into the kitchen with wide eyes, holding a big envelope.

"Look at this. It's from the Angels and it's for Laura. Let's open it."

I hadn't planned on this. I didn't really think that Jim Abbott would write back.

"We can't do that. It's addressed to Laura. We'll have to wait till she gets home."

I feel terrible. David stares at the envelope.

"What can it be? Maybe some pictures of the Angels, or some sticker, but why is it addressed to Laura? I just can't figure it out." Dave doesn't want to put the envelope down.

"I need to pick up Laura from school. I'll be just a few minutes."

As Laura gets to the car, I can't wait to tell her. "Guess what! You got a letter from the Angels."

"Jim Abbott?" Her whole face lights up. "But you told me he wouldn't write for weeks, or maybe not at all."

"Guess I was wrong." I smile. "And Dave's home, too. He can't figure out what you're getting from the Angels."

"Oh good," Laura laughs. "I can hardly wait to see his face. He'll be so excited. It's really for him."

So we race home and Laura rushes in the house.

"Oh Laura," I say as calmly as possible. "There's some mail for you."

"Who's it from?"

"It says the Angels."

With David hanging over her shoulder, ready to grab the envelope and tear it open himself, Laura slowly opens the envelope.

"Look, Mom, it's a letter from Jim Abbott and a signed photograph."

"Here, let me read it to you. It says, 'Thank you for the letter…'"

"What letter?" David blurts out.

Laura can hardly wait to tell him. "Oh Dave, that was the fun. We wrote a letter to Jim Abbott last week at your ballgame, and gave Mike the letter, but I really didn't think he'd write back."

Dave sits down and reads the letter carefully and looks at the signed photograph. "This is so neat. He really wrote to you. Wow."

"Dave, why don't you call Mike and tell him what we got?"

Mike talks to a reporter from the *LA Times*, who wants to do a story about Laura and Jim Abbott. I thank Mike, but writing the letter was never for publicity. We've had enough newspaper articles and interviews.

But Mike is persistent, and by July I give in. A journalist comes and takes pictures of Laura and writes a very nice article for the Sunday paper. I was hoping that David and Laura could meet Jim Abbott, but it's a story about Laura, not an interview with him.

On Monday morning the phone rings early.

"My name is Steve," a man says. "I'm a photographer with the Angels. It sounds like Laura would like to meet Jim Abbott."

"Well, yes, she'd love to."

"If you get tickets to a game that he's pitching, I'll make sure you get down in the dugout to meet him. Call me when you have the tickets." He gives me his name and phone number.

I'm thrilled when I hang up the phone, but then I start worrying. Who is this person? Is he really with the Angels? He could be some nut calling just because he read the article in the paper. I call Don at his office.

"What if we get to Angel Stadium and he's not there?" I ask him.

Don is very logical. "The worst that'll happen is that we get tickets to an Angels game with Abbott pitching. That won't be so bad."

"But it would be a terrible disappointment for the kids."

"We'll just have to tell them that's a possibility."

I buy the tickets, and call Steve back to arrange the meeting.

"Do you think that someone can go with Laura to meet Jim Abbott?" I'm crossing my fingers. David has to be able to meet him.

"One pass is usually all I can get. Why?"

"Laura would feel a lot more comfortable if her brother could come with her."

"Well, I'll try to get two, but I'm not sure."

I thank him again and hang up the phone.

June 28, 1989

A few weeks later we drive to Angel Stadium. Dave is bursting with excitement at the thought of meeting Jim Abbott. I wish I could feel as positive. I'll feel terrible if he can't. More than terrible. It would be so unfair to David. Laura constantly gets all the attention and now even in baseball, she's captured the attention. It's my fault for even suggesting the letter. David just can't be left out this time!

A TV truck pulls up at our designated meeting spot right outside the entrance, and a man gets out.

"Hi, I'm Steve. It's good to meet you."

I'm afraid to ask.

Steve reaches into his pocket. "I got two passes for Laura and, I'm sorry, I don't know his name."

"David," I say quickly as David stands anxiously behind us.

I breathe a sigh of relief as Steve walks with my children down the long underground corridor leading to the stadium. He shows the guard his photographer's pass, and they disappear into the darkness. I watch for a few more seconds, wondering belatedly if I've taught them to be polite, and if they'll know what to say and how to say it.

I'd love to meet Jim Abbott, too. I admire him. He was born with an unformed right hand, and he's become a pitcher with a major league team. He's beaten incredible odds to get where he is today, and I can't imagine that kind of courage and determination, except in my own little girl.

We find our seats by right field, where we can see the dugout. The Angels are practicing on the field, and I see some very small figures waiting in the dugout, one with a bright green skirt. My kids. My heart beats quickly.

The Angels start coming in from the field. Someone sits next to David, and motions for another to come over. I can only imagine how excited they are.

Jim Abbott isn't off the field yet. I'm sure David is having everyone sign his baseball. Then I see Abbott go into the dugout. He crouches down in front of them, probably signing a baseball. He stands, but instead of leaving, he sits down next to them.

The kids are down in the dugout for over an hour, while Don and I squint to see what's happening. Finally we can't wait anymore, and we walk closer to home plate so we can see better. Laura spots us, and pretty soon she and Jim Abbott walk over. We get to meet him for a few minutes, then everyone in the seats around us starts yelling, "Jim! Jim!"

Don and I go back, but Laura and Dave and Abbott return to the dugout. Pretty soon I spot a little green skirt moving toward us, half a field away. We go out to meet Steve and the kids.

"I had no idea they would get to stay for so long. Thank you so much."

David and Laura are bubbling with excitement. "We met everybody, mom. Jim Abbott and Wally Joyner and Chili Davis and everybody! Look, they signed our baseballs and Jim Abbott gave me another picture."

When we get home the kids talk into the night and on to the next day, barely stopping to sleep. We frame the letter with a picture of Jim Abbott and Laura that Steve took in the dugout.

Chapter 22

Laura and Ebony

Credit: Los Angeles Times

July 10, 1989

I haven't played the piano in front of an audience in almost two years, but Linda asks me to play at a Catholic church by Leisure World, and I want to try. Three simple hymns are all I have to play.

I flip on the light switch, walk up the steep steps to the musty choir loft, and turn on the organ. I hate organs. I know I can do this. It's a Benediction service, and with my heart beating quickly and my fingers clammy, I play the first hymn as the priest walks out to the altar. Just one verse. That's all they want.

There are only about ten people down below. I get to the end of the hymn. I did it.

The second hymn comes after the short sermon. And then the final hymn, "Holy God, We Praise Thy Name." I can't hear anyone singing, and I don't think it's because I'm too loud. I turn off the organ and lock the choir loft.

I guess my friend was right. Life is getting better, and I'm not as afraid to play anymore. I don't like the service. It's a very traditional service that somehow missed all the reforms of the church. But it's simple and pays well. I feel bad that Don is completely responsible for supporting us.

September 1989

Sid Weiss, Laura's eye doctor, meets me at his temple's choir practice. In the three years since the attack, we've gotten to know Sid pretty well. He's come to our house for dinner, and we spent the weekend with him at a condo up in Big Bear, a mountain resort. He doesn't have a family of his own yet, but he wants one. I feel special to be his friend. He's a wonderful, caring person, and the kids both love him. He's always making bets with them about learning things, and he never pays his extravagant promises when the kids actually win the bet. But they don't care. It's all a game.

Sid convinces me to play for his temple choir. I fall in love with the Jewish folk songs and the Jewish attitude toward God.

After practice, Sid tells me he needs to get home quickly because he's picked up a dog at the shelter and it's out in his Porsche. We walk out together. He opens the car door and a silly black puppy runs over to me. As I kneel down, the puppy puts its head on my knee and sighs. I'm in love. I've never seen such a cute dog. He has curly black hair. I ask Sid if we can babysit the dog when he goes out of town.

I'm sure Sid doesn't believe me about the dog sitting. Laura is deathly afraid of dogs because of the attack, but I hate for her to be so fearful. I ask her if I can babysit this cute little puppy, and she says yes, but only if he stays outside.

A few weeks later, Sid asks us to watch Ebony. All Saturday morning, Laura's face is pressed up against the sliding glass door with Ebony on the other side. She wants to be with him, but she's so afraid. Ebony whines and paws at the door.

I ask Laura if we can let the dog in, but protect her on the couch behind lots of pillows. She agrees. So Ebony bounces in and Laura hides behind the cushions. She reaches out and touches him from her safe place. It takes about three minutes for the cushions to fall over, and then Ebony is sitting on her lap and he's licking her face and they're the best of friends.

I'm thrilled. I wouldn't want Laura to hate all animals because of the mountain lion, but I'm glad to see Ebony go back home on Sunday night. I don't want a full-time dog. So every time Sid goes out of town, we watch his dog, and grow to love him. Of course, I loved him from the first minute I saw him.

One Saturday morning, I call Sid to ask him about choir practice.

"Wow, it's really strange that you called this morning."

"Why?"

"Well, I'm just about to take Ebony back to the shelter. It's not working out. I have to be gone too often, and my girlfriend says it's either me or the dog. I think I want to keep the girlfriend."

"You can't take him to the shelter. We want him."

"No you don't. You made it really clear that you just wanted him for a few weekends. I know you don't want him full time. You told me that."

"I know, but I don't want him to go to the shelter. Don't leave yet. I'll call you back in five minutes. Honestly. Stay. Five minutes."

As I hang up the phone, I yell, "Hey, everybody, get out here in the kitchen. Emergency meeting!"

Dave opens the door of his room and peers out. Don walks to the kitchen from the computer room. Laura runs in holding a paintbrush.

"Sid is taking Ebony to the animal shelter this morning."

"What?" "He can't do that!" "We have to take him." "Please, Mom."

Don finally says, realistically, "I'm not sure that we want a full time dog."

211

But Don can't possibly win this one, with the three of us squirming and whining next to him. Besides, he loves Ebony too. He just has to be practical.

I call Sid back in less than three minutes. "We're taking him."

"I'm serious. I can't take him back. This wasn't an easy decision."

"I know. If it doesn't work out, we'll bring him to the shelter ourselves. You don't have to worry about it."

"Are you sure?"

"Yes."

So we pick up Ebony and bring him home. Our new guard dog is not very frightening. He's a thirty-pound cocker spaniel mix with floppy black ears. He has spindly legs and feet that look like a cross between a Hobbit and a Dr. Seuss animal. He wants to be a lap dog but some part of him always hangs over the couch. He barks loudly when anyone comes to the door, but all a burglar would have to do is reach down and pet him and he'd love them wildly.

He follows us all over the house; he's warm at night with his head in my lap. Within a few weeks, I can't imagine our lives without him.

November 1989

The priest is mumbling through his sermon; David sighs on the bench next to me, and Laura closes her eyes. My eyes wander to the high vaulted ceiling with the chandeliers hanging from long steel cords. I think about the last earthquake, and I wonder how quickly the unsupported ceiling would crumble.

I've been on firm ground all my life, the belief in God like a rock beneath my feet, but now my faith is in earthquake country. Laura's alive and well, and I should be immensely grateful to God. But I'm not. There are so many who suffer, and so many random events that strike people, I wonder if there's really anyone in charge.

I don't know exactly why I'm returning to church, except that my loss of faith has torn apart my life, and I can't see how my unbelief will bring me anything but sorrow. The thought of no afterlife is terrifying. Never seeing anyone after they die is profoundly sad. I'm not ready to turn my back on all that just yet. I have to give my faith every chance I can.

Surprisingly, it's Laura who questions God the most.

As we leave church, Laura asks, "Why don't animals have souls?" I vaguely remember the priest saying something about animals and souls, before my mind wandered to the ceiling and earthquakes.

"Aren't they at the level of a little baby, and babies have souls? And what about dolphins and whales and the gorilla that learned all those words in sign language? And I know Ebony has a soul."

I don't have an answer for her.

A week later, I'm practicing the psalm, "I will sing to my God, who delivers me from death…" It refers to the deliverance of the Hebrews and the destruction of the Egyptians who died following Moses through the Red Sea.

Laura's incensed with that. "What about the Egyptians? He just killed them? They were people he created. That's terrible."

I try to explain that it's a story showing the power of God. Then Laura reads about the first-born child of the Egyptians being killed.

"There's no excuse for that," she says vehemently. "If that's the way God is, I don't like him."

We talk about the book of Job. Laura's angry about that too, the way God treated Job like a game. I assure her it's just a story, and that God isn't really like he's portrayed in the Old Testament. He's more merciful and kind. But I wonder. So many terrible and cruel things happen to people. Maybe he isn't kind or merciful.

I can't remember one time I ever doubted God before Laura's attack. I see myself at six, lying in bed, listening to the breathing of my two older sisters, thinking about eternity. We had learned from Sister Angeline, her fat red face squeezed into the tight-fitting veil, that we were here on earth to love and serve God, and then to be happy with him in heaven. Right out of the Catholic Baltimore Catechism. I lay tiny under the covers, barely able to see the porch light through the slats of the blinds, listening to the rain, and wondering how anyone could be happy for such a long time. I tried to think about eating ice cream, like Sister had suggested, but doing that hour after hour for all eternity seemed boring. I worried about eternity a lot, and I worried about whether I'd be happy with God, but I never doubted his existence.

In high school I decided that the Catholic Church didn't know much more than I did, partly because I was a typical teenager. But I always knew someone was out there, loving us, caring for us, and wanting us to be in heaven with him someday.

My faith wasn't any great accomplishment. It wasn't like practicing the piano and getting better each week. Everyone I knew believed in God. My parents and grandparents and sisters and aunts and uncles and cousins and friends, all Irish Catholics with a few German Protestants, believed in God. It never occurred to me not to believe.

The word atheist was a bad word, all tied up with Communism, and both were horrible threats to our country and world. I could never be like that. "Godless Communists," described people who were mean and cruel and had no morals at all, like Stalin and Lenin. Hitler got thrown in there too, although I was too young to know that he wasn't an atheist or a Communist.

Don was the first atheist I ever met. I was surprised that he was kind and caring, and would never tell a lie. We talked about our income tax returns soon after I met him, and I was trying to find a way to pay less money. Don was surprised. He would never lie—about anything. I thought that all morals were from God, but I began to realize that godless people could be good, honest people.

Even when I married Don, my faith wasn't shaken. Don knew science and math, but his experience with religion had prevented him from knowing God. I hoped that someday he would see the light.

Now I'm the one doubting, going to church every week and cynically examining every long-held belief. There wasn't one that held up to the light of reason. From original sin to the Virgin birth, from God's all-powerful status to the reality that He was not in control of evil. The list was endless.

I sit in the church pew a week later with David and Laura on either side. We sing "Amazing Grace" as the parishioners shuffle in a steady line to receive Communion. I sing the words to be a good example to my children. "I once was lost, but now am found, was blind, but now I see."

I've always loved "Amazing Grace," but what if I've been blind, because I believed in someone who never even existed? What if the reality is that our existence is but a brief moment, and then gone? What if I was blind, and now I can see?

Chapter 23

Laura with ballet teacher

Credit: Los Angeles Times

December 1989

The county has decided, after three years, to take our depositions. Wylie wants to meet with us to prepare for them.

I'm standing in Wylie's office looking at his Christmas tree. It towers over the large reception area. The ornaments are elegant, covered with white lace. White lights twinkle through the green branches.

Our tree at home is a little off-center, but it was the best one I could find at Home Depot. The branches on one side are sparse, so we just hang more ornaments on that side. We have quite a collection, from the kid's homemade school creations, the Eveready bunny series from Carl's Jr., and mooing cows. Star Wars battleships hide between branches and a woven star from Kenya tops it off. I like our tree better.

The secretary smiles. "Mr. Aitken wants you to come right back. Your husband is in there already."

The secretary walks back with me along the thick Oriental rugs that line the corridor. I sit down next to Don and listen to Wylie.

"You'll need to answer all the questions, unless I raise an objection. Don't get long winded and volunteer more information. The depositions are for the county's information, not ours. If I have any questions, I can ask you in here, in my office."

"Describe to me exactly what you saw or heard, Don, because I'm sure the county will try to get you out when they realize you didn't see the lion."

Wylie feels that since Don had been there, heard my screams and tried desperately to find Laura, that he had a "contemporaneous sensory experience," and that he should be allowed to collect damages. But the county will latch onto the fact that Don hadn't seen the lion.

Why should a technicality ruin Don's chances for collecting any damages? He had been a few hundred feet down the trail. He suffered as much as I did, even though he did not see the actual moment of the attack. He ran frantically through the brush to find Laura, and he saw her seconds after Greg beat off the lion. He held her as we ran up the dirt road for help. He had been with her and stayed with her and cried about her. But that wasn't enough. He needed to have one little glimpse of the mountain lion. How absurd.

A few days later I return to Wylie's office. My deposition is first. Wylie and I walk to the conference room. This is the first time I've told the story to the county, and it will be hard not to describe the events in great detail. I felt so confident and righteous yesterday. But as I walk down the corridor with Wylie, my confidence slips away. I know nothing about this game, and the lawyers are experts at it.

A big, hulking man is standing next to a woman in the conference room.

Wylie smiles at them. The man steps forward and holds out a large fleshy hand for me to shake.

"Mrs. Small, I'm Barry Allen, the lawyer from the county. This is Susan, my associate."

I find it difficult to make my mouth go up at the edges. The veneer of civility is very thin. I hate these people. I hate what they've done to us. And yet, I'm shaking hands and saying "Good morning," when what I really want to do is start hitting them in a fury because of the last three years.

My stomach feels like lead and my hands are clammy as we sit down on opposite sides of the large conference table. Wylie sits next to me, still smiling. We chat for a few minutes and Barry Allen says that it's nice to finally meet me.

Nice? I don't know what to say, so I say nothing. I certainly don't feel it's nice to meet him! This is the same man who has made our lives so difficult. He sits with a condescending smile, ready to use everything I say against me.

His first question is about Don's business. Don had written an optical design program and we were selling his software program before the attack. I said I was an active partner.

"What, exactly, is the optical program about?"

My role as an active partner was answering the telephone from home, taking orders, xeroxing the program, packing it, and mailing it to the customer. I have no idea how to explain the optical design program. I can't even answer the first question. I feel like an idiot, but he keeps on asking me questions about the program, even though I'm basically a secretary.

This is a chess game, and I'm trying to think a few moves ahead. But depositions aren't my game, and I'm at a disadvantage. The only thing going for me is that I'm telling the truth and I have nothing to hide. That doesn't make my stomach feel any better, though, as I sit there with my sweaty hands folded in my lap.

I see Allen across the table, listening intently to my replies. I feel Wylie next to me, calm and steady.

The large shiny conference table stretches wide and long, taking up almost the entire room. The plush carpets and subdued lighting give a false sense of security and warmth. I have to be on my guard.

Allen abruptly switches the subject.

"About how many times did you go to Casper's Park?"

I stutter a vague reply because we had been going there for years, even before Laura was born. I have no idea how many times we had been there. I sound like an idiot.

"What does Laura complain about to you on a regular basis?"

"Complain about?" Laura complains so little. She doesn't complain about her eye, which is her severest injury. She doesn't remember what it was like to have both eyes. She doesn't complain about the aplastic anemia, which almost killed her. I want to tell him how Laura has suffered, about how our lives had totally fallen apart, and we tried to keep picking up the pieces. No, he doesn't want to hear about that.

I want to say, "You bastard. You wait three years after the accident till we're all doing better, then you ask what Laura complains about." The fact that she doesn't complain and has such a positive attitude now seems a disadvantage. My anger, which has been simmering all morning, nearly boils over in frustration.

But I think about Wylie and how he never gets angry, and I mutter something about how Laura doesn't complain very much, but she still has severe injuries.

Barry Allen, toward the end of the four and a half hours of questioning, asks, "Do you feel Laura has any special talents or abilities?"

I sit there silently, picturing her at ballet class, trying so hard to lift her arms. What talent would she have had if she hadn't been hurt? And music. Would I have taught her the piano? I always wanted to. She can't even use her right hand.

And all those talents she might have been developing if she didn't have to spend her time at doctor's appointments and therapy sessions. Tears come to my eyes when I think of how beautifully talented she was and is, and what might have been.

Barry Allen is trying to trick me, trying to make me say that she's talented and can do all those things that other girls her age can do, and then use it against me in the courtroom.

He repeats the question. "Do you feel Laura has any special talents or abilities?"

I say very softly, "No."

"I'm sorry, I didn't hear the answer."

"No, I don't think she has any special talents."

But as I say no, I feel like I've betrayed Laura. I've reached out again to grab her, and I've missed again, because in my heart I know that she's talented and gifted, a rare jewel of a child.

She has grown into a caring little girl who doesn't have the heart to kill any living creature. Spiders need to be lifted carefully on a piece of paper and placed outside. Maybe it's a realization of how precious and fragile life is, from one who knows.

She is smart. She reads on a higher level than most children her age and loves books. Her ballet lessons are mostly for therapy and to meet other children. She'll never learn to play the piano, or cello, or the bagpipes, which she would really love to learn.

But she can draw with her left hand, and she's becoming quite a good artist.

She's cheerful and happy, kind and caring. She never complains. She loves animals more than people. Animals can't make fun of her. They can't make rude comments about how she looks or how different she is. But even though her life is made difficult by her classmates, she has a bright smile and a happy outlook on life. I wouldn't trade her for anyone in the world. She is my entire world.

I hate Barry Allen for making me say that she has no special talents. No, he didn't make me say anything. I hate myself for saying it. I tell Laura silently that I'll make this up to her, again.

The deposition drags on, the subjects changing rapidly, and then Allen turns to me.

"Does Laura look normal?" I can barely answer him. What kind of a question is that to ask?

I go home exhausted. Don and I talk that night about the horrible questions. His deposition is in the morning.

I tell him one last time, "I know you don't want to lie. And I do want you to do what's right. But that law is wrong, when it says you have to actually see the mountain lion. You suffered as much as I did. It's just not right. Anyway, none of us know what you saw. You're the only one."

Don listens to me quietly.

"I feel that the law is wrong too. But the truth is that I didn't see the lion. Even if I'm the only one that knows that, it's still what happened. I can't lie about it."

Don's deposition starts at 10:00 the next morning. He doesn't get home till 7:00 that evening.

"How was it?" I ask as he comes in the door.

"Horrible." I know how he feels. Like someone has drained all the blood out of you a drop at a time.

"What did you say about seeing the lion?"

"I didn't see the lion. They asked me and that's what I told them. What's there to eat? I'm starving."

After we go to bed, I lie awake and think about Don. I feel that we live in two separate worlds. But tonight I realize again why I married him and why I still love him. He's a good honest person.

Good and honest. When Don asked me to marry him years ago, I hadn't even been out of the convent a whole year. I wasn't really interested in getting married. So I said no, not once, but quite a few times. Six months later he asked,

"What would you say if I asked you to marry me?"

My resistance was worn down. "I'd probably say yes."

That was the proposal. I was so afraid of losing my new independence that I almost lost Don. Good and honest. That's what he was. Not flashy, not rich. He loved to hike-I didn't. He didn't talk much. But there was something about him that I could sense. A kindness, much like my father and grandfather. A good heart. Someone who would always be there for me, as I would for him.

I wonder if I would have had the courage to tell the truth. I did tell the truth at my deposition, but I had everything to gain. There was no great moral judgment to make. I wonder with all my Christian morality, if I would have been as brave and honest as my atheist husband.

The county puts in a motion for summary judgment, which means they're trying to get Don removed from the lawsuit. We hold our breath till the court date arrives.

Wylie argues that because Don heard my screams, searched frantically for Laura, saw her seconds after the lion released her, and was there hearing and reacting to my screams, that he should be part of the lawsuit. He argues that a blind person, by that same reasoning, could never collect damages, if seeing was the only way a person could be present.

We wait over a month for the ruling, and the judge agrees with Wylie. Don is able to remain in the case.

I breathe a huge sigh of relief. Don seems pleased. It's a victory I keep to myself. I hate to admit that I might have lied about it. The ruling goes virtually unnoticed in the long line of small court victories. But it makes me wake up to some qualities about Don that I had all but forgotten in the rush of our lives, and how much I really do love him.

Chapter 24

February 13, 1990

The rain drips steadily from the eaves, a grey cool day. I'm straightening up Laura's room, putting away a few presents from her birthday party. I hang up a dress and spread the blanket on her bed, both chores that are still difficult for her. I wish she could use her right hand and arm. Even though she's managed amazingly well over the last few years, there are so many things she can't do. Button clothes, play a musical instrument, open a can of soda, turn a doorknob. As I hang up her pink dress, the phone rings. It's Wylie's secretary.

"Wylie got a call from Larry King today, and they'd like you and Don and Laura to be on the show next week. Wylie wants to know if you're interested. Call and let us know. It would be at the studios out here in LA, not in Washington, D.C."

I know what prompted the call. Laura's tenth birthday was a few days before, on February 10th. That same day the county had reopened Casper's Park to adults, but not children. No children were allowed in the park. Everyone was angry with us. I read about it in both Orange County newspapers. All the TV channels carried the story, with interviews from irate citizens who felt the county had no right to deny anyone access to the park.

As their answer, the county pointed to us.

"If it weren't for their lawsuit, we wouldn't have to keep children out of the park!" Their statement was released to the Los Angeles Times, all the local news channels, and the Associated Press, which fed it to news outlets all over the country.

We always felt that if people are warned about the dangers, then it's their responsibility to decide whether to go in the park. Don and I are furious that the county made this ruling on Laura's birthday. It was no accident.

Don, the introvert, doesn't want to be on Larry King, but Wylie and I are excited. I plead with Laura to go on the show. A few bribes help. The show is scheduled for the next Wednesday, and we'll meet up at Wylie's office. A limo will bring us to the Los Angeles studios in time for make-up and a quick meeting with the producers. I've never ridden in a limo, and it sounds more and more fun as the week goes on.

Doctor's appointments, therapy, more surgeries, and the endless lawsuit have consumed my life. Going on the show sounds exciting. I should be worried, but I'm not. Wylie will be there and he'll do most of the talking. I find out Henry Winkler will be on the segment after us, and we might even get to meet him.

The afternoon before the taping, I pick up Laura from school. "Guess who we're going to meet on the Larry King show tomorrow? Henry Winkler, the guy who plays the Fonz on Happy Days!"

She looks at me blankly. "Who?"

"You know, the show, 'Happy Days'?"

"No."

I can't believe she's never seen the show. It's true that I've never sat down with her to watch it. But the kids watch shows on the cartoon channel during the day, and I just assumed that they had seen it.

When Dave gets home from skateboarding, I tell him, "Guess who we're going to meet tomorrow? The Fonz. Henry Winkler. From Happy Days."

"Who?"

Dave hasn't heard of him either. My generation has come and gone. Reruns on Nickleodeon aren't enough to bring back an era. It's too late to run to the movie store to get out reruns of Happy Days, but I feel bad that Laura won't know whom she's meeting.

Don goes with us, even though he won't be on the show. The limo never arrives the afternoon of the Larry King show, so we jump in Wylie's Bronco. Don drives, weaving through the Los Angeles rush hour traffic, and we pull up late to the studio, just a few minutes before six. Someone pushes me into the make-up room and another person goes with Laura. When we're ushered out of the room we see Henry Winkler. We have a fast introduction and say hello. I'm thrilled to meet him. He seems nice in the 30 seconds we get to talk, and then we get rushed into the studio. We sit behind a long desk and three people are next to us, attaching headphones and a microphone.

A man explains quickly that we won't actually see Larry King, not even on the TV monitor. We need to look directly at the white lens across the room when we're answering his questions. That's Larry King to us. There's a three second delay to weed out any expletives, so make sure we listen in our headphones, not up on the monitors directly above us. Someone asks Laura a question but she can't hear it. They come over and turn the volume up but I'm not sure it's right. But then they give us the signal, and begin counting down: 5, 4, 3. Then two fingers, then one. The show begins.

Larry King introduces us, and I have a hard time remembering who I am. The lights are glaring and I can barely hear him in the monitors. I must have a weird look on my face. I want to relax but I'm having a hard time concentrating on what he's saying. I tell what happened to Laura that day at the park. Wylie takes a question and I try to smile. Laura doesn't hear the question that Larry King asks and she asks him to repeat it. Finally she answers. Wylie talks again about the responsibility of the park. I'm asked another question and I feel like I'm talking to a point of distant light, which doesn't care what I'm saying. We take a break for a commercial. I ask them to adjust Laura's monitor for volume. I think it's better for her now. We smile and say we're ready. It doesn't matter. Now there are questions being called in.

"What if someone were attacked by a diseased rabbit on the streets of Los Angeles. Would you hold the city responsible for that?"

I don't even answer the idiotic question. I take the opportunity to talk about the responsibility of the county and how they neglected to warn us about a danger that they were well aware of. I nail the answer to that one. Unfortunately, now that I'm all warmed up, it's over. The time is up and we take off the microphones and shake the hands of people in the studio, thanking them.

We go back out to the holding room and Don says we did just fine, but I don't believe him. I feel like I've been hiking for hours under a hot desert sun.

Wylie talks a lot on the way home, but I feel exhausted. Someone tapes the show for us and I watch it once. I guess I did ok. Laura sounded like she couldn't understand the questions. My mom says that I looked like I had a gun to my head, which was a pretty accurate description of how I felt.

No more talk shows. My sense of adventure goes into hiding, and I'm satisfied to sit at home.

Chapter 25

September 13, 1990

The ringing of the phone blends seamlessly into my dream. But it doesn't stop. Suddenly I'm awake, heart pounding. I grope for the phone in the darkness.

My sister Carol, her voice shaking, says, "Sue, Dad's dead."

"What?"

"I'm at Mom's. He died last night in his sleep. When she woke up this morning she tried to get him up but couldn't."

Just like that, I'm fully awake. "Is Mom ok?" I don't know what else to ask. Tears start welling up in my eyes.

"She's ok. I'll call you as soon as I know anything more."

I struggle to get the phone back in the receiver and turn to Don, who's sitting up beside me.

"Dad's dead. He didn't wake up this morning. Carol's at the apartment with mom." And then I can't get any more words out because I'm crying. Don hugs me and we get up.

I fly back to St. Louis with the children. Don can't because of work. I stay at my mom's, and she is doing as well as possible. She had a lot of trouble with dad's loss of memory. I remember how it was when they were out here after Laura's attack, when he couldn't even remember she'd been attacked. But he still talked about tennis and worked his crossword puzzles. Mom said the night he died, they sat outside and talked, enjoying the cool fall evening.

My dad's funeral is in mom's Catholic church. My dad never went there.

It's an old dark church that's trying to be modern, like so many Catholic churches built in the fifties. The wooden cross hangs over the carved altar with the modern granite altar in front. All my relatives are there, my sisters and nieces and nephew, and a few old friends of the family. Laura holds my hand and cries quietly. The coffin is wheeled to the altar. The organist starts playing and a man sings, "On Eagles Wings." My dad probably never heard the piece in his whole life.

Even though I play at funerals, I have a hard time connecting this service with my father. It wasn't like him to be in a dark stuffy church. If my dad has a soul that lives on, it's out on the tennis courts, in the cool breeze.

I open the music book and try to sing so I don't have to think. Then the service is over and I help mom down the aisle after the coffin. She's doing ok. She's a strong woman. We drive to the gravesite for a short ceremony.

We stay at my mom's for a few days. David and Laura are quiet and shy, and don't know what to say. School has just started and we have to get back to California.

Back home, I'm out of step, like I stumbled and haven't caught up to others. No one knew my father. No one cares about him or remembers him. Something feels wrong with my life.

My dad and I were never close. We never talked about how we felt, or any kind of emotion. He laughed a lot, and played tennis, and talked about politics. He had lots of stories about his life in Germany and his early years in the United States, but we never really talked about anything personal. He was a happy man, quite content in the world. He used to ask me, "Are you happy?" And I always said I was. And that was it. He was content to know that much, and didn't need to know anything else. Maybe that's all we really need to know about each other.

Whenever I called home, I'd talk to mom. Sometimes he'd answer the phone and we'd have a short conversation before he handed the phone to my mom. Like many other men, he had trouble expressing emotions. I don't think it occurred to him to have long heart to heart talks with any of his daughters. He wouldn't have known what to say.

He taught me by example. He would play tennis with anyone, regardless of color or religion. He played with his Christian friends on Saturday and his Jewish friends on Sunday. He played with Arthur Ashe, the great black tennis champion, when Ashe was a high school student in St. Louis. I remember Dad telling us to watch for Ashe in the news, because he was so good. Dad was quite a tennis champion in his time. He won the Missouri state championship the year I was born, and would have gone on to others, if we'd had the money. Tennis was not lucrative like it is today. So he kept his regular job and played for fun.

He was invited to join country clubs in the St. Louis area, but he refused. He was perfectly happy on the city courts, where he could play with anyone, black or white, and hated the fact that blacks were excluded. He didn't want to have anything to do with those racist organizations.

One day in October, a month after the funeral, as I'm weeding outside, I think of going to an ice cream store with my dad when I was young. We would walk there in the humid summer evenings to buy ice cream. I was five or six, and dad would stand next to me, buying the cones at Velvet Freeze and sitting in the red vinyl booth while we ate, the cold strawberry ice cream melting on my tongue, my feet not reaching the linoleum floor.

I start crying then, all the tears I haven't cried. It isn't the Strauss waltzes that bring him back, or the tennis he loved, or the wooden puzzles he made, or any of those things. It's the memory of an ice cream store. Funny, it's all the little things that do matter in the end.

November 5, 1990

Don suggested a few months ago that I read a book called *The Blind Watchmaker* by Richard Dawkins, a famous evolutionary biologist. He thought I might like it.

I remember the watchmaker story well. My mom was going to college when I was in high school. She had been teaching for years in a Catholic grade school and decided to get her teaching credential. One evening we were both studying at the kitchen table.

She looked up from her book.

"I heard a really interesting story today from my professor. Imagine that there's a desert island and one day a little metal part of a watch washes up in the tide and is deposited on the beach. Then a million years later a tiny spring washes up on the same beach. Every million years another little part washes up on the beach and one day the watch starts ticking. That's pretty unbelievable. It's laughable that could ever happen. And that's how impossible it is to believe that this world came into existence without a creator."

I remember being impressed by the story all those years ago. And Don says that is the story referred to in the title, *The Blind Watchmaker*. I wonder how the author will explain evolution without God, because I do know he is a famous atheist.

I can't put the book down. What I read changes my life. Someone else has asked all the questions I've been asking about the existence of God, and has come up with the same answers. I read the book again and talk to Don about it. He's the only one I can talk to about all these questions, although he doesn't care nearly as much as I do. He's already lived a whole lifetime not believing in God, and has always wondered why anybody believes in God.

I lie in bed and think about God, just like a thousand other nights. I've been sitting on the fence between belief and non-belief for so long. I want to make a decision. The broken record of "Is there a God or isn't there a God?" echoes through my dreams every night, but I can't decide. I want to believe someone has control over this universe. I want to believe in an afterlife. They've been part of my whole existence, and I can't imagine life without believing. But I'm increasingly dissatisfied with all the simplistic platitudes that don't really answer the questions.

If we are so complex that we had to be created by someone, then God, the most complex being, couldn't just have sprung into existence without being created. He's an infinite, perfect, all-powerful, all-knowing, transcendent, eternal being who just exists and created everything out of nothing-oh, and loves us personally. Now that's hard to believe. No, impossible to believe.

I've believed in evolution since I was a freshman in high school and read many of the great Catholic theologians, especially de Chardin, who wrote about evolution. We can see changes in species in our own short lifetimes. The variety of dogs is just one example. Given billions of years, we see the results when we look at all the incredible variety of life on our planet. But then we throw this infinite perfect being into the equation, the creator who was never created. The complex being who came from nowhere and is eternal. It just doesn't follow any rule of logic. Dawkins asks the question I've always wondered about, "Who created God?"

So it isn't that I'm tired of listening to boring sermons, or condescending priests, or ridiculous rules of the church, although those have all been part of my

Catholic experience. My biggest problem is that I can't believe there is a God. If there is one, then I'm fine with Jesus and the church and the priests and the sacraments and original sin and miracles and fish on Friday. Whatever God wants is fine with me. I just don't think there is a God.

I'm going against thousands of years of belief. I know I'm not smarter than the very great minds of the past and the present. But, after reading Dawkins book, I know that other people have asked these same questions, and I know I'm not alone anymore.

I'm so close to not believing, but it's frightening. I can't even imagine that safety net being taken away. I wish I could decide. I wish I could know for sure. I'm the needle on the record, stuck at the end, the scratchy sound repeated over and over.

April 1991

I'm at church with David and Laura on Holy Saturday, the night of the Easter Vigil. Ever since I was young, I've loved the vigil, with its candles and themes of light and darkness. The music is so ancient and beautiful. But all the Easters since Laura's attack have been frustrating because of my constant struggle with my faith.

I walk into church feeling I should have learned something. In the four years since Laura's attack I've been beating my head against a wall, trying to find answers. And I have nothing. Not the simple answers of my childhood, or the more complex theology of the convent years. I feel so maddeningly frustrated.

The night is surprisingly warm, and the lights in the church are slowly dimmed. We light our candles from the Paschal candle, the large candle that symbolizes the light of Christ. Whether I believe or not, it is a truly beautiful service. Plus, people look better in candlelight.

I watch David light Laura's candle, hoping they won't set someone's hair on fire.

Laura looks beautiful by candlelight. Her hair is wrapped around her head in a long braid, and even though it was bought at the wig place, it looks like her own. David, my little boy, is now fourteen, taller than Don. We sing during the liturgy and then the baptisms start. There are five babies and even more adults. After the baptisms, the priest says to the congregation, "Please answer 'I do' after each question."

"Do you renounce Satan and all his works?"

I do.

"Do you believe in God?"

I do.

"Do you believe in Jesus Christ…"

As I stand there, all alone in the overflowing church, I realize I can't go on mouthing words I don't believe.

I'm angry. I've tried so hard to understand. I agonized over Laura's attack and her recovery. I've asked why. And I'm no closer to the truth than when I was five years old. And then just as suddenly I know that I'll never understand. I'll never know for sure if God exists. And there isn't one person who has any more answers than I do.

The blackness is ahead of me. I have reached the edge of the cliff. I could step back and go over all this again, read more books, listen to more sermons. I can stay where I am, asking the same questions over and over. Or I can step off into the complete darkness. That's what it feels like at this moment in this stuffy church with the incense drifting over the congregation like a cloud.

And so, after four years of doubt and questioning, I step into the darkness of unbelief. How strange that I should decide during the Easter Vigil, that holiest of days. A sense of freedom and terror surrounds me. But I'm still falling, and even though I reach out to grab onto something, there's nothing there.

The service is over. David is anxious to leave. Laura is sleepy. My faith is like the candle, extinguished, thrown on the wooden seat, to be picked up and thrown away. I walk outside and take a deep breath of the brisk night air. I don't know what's next, but I know there's no going back.

Chapter 26

May 2, 1991

Laura's hair has grown since the last operation to put the Lexan plate in her head, but there are large skin grafts where the hair won't grow. Dr. Watanabe wants to stretch the skin on her scalp again to give her more hair-growing areas. Laura's in fifth grade now. There's no reason to put off this last operation. Her blood count has stabilized, although it continues to be low. We decide to go ahead with the operation. The summer will be the worst time, but she won't be in school, and hopefully they can operate before she begins sixth grade.

May 13, 1991

The trial is finally set for June of 1991. Because Mike and Rich have done all the preliminary work on it, I still worry that Wylie isn't prepared. Yes, he won that motion for Don's dismissal from the case, but he doesn't know our lawsuit as well as he should.

Losing is too horrible to contemplate. I don't want to be bitter, always complaining about the unfairness of life. I try to focus on winning.

An article appears in the *LA Times* outlining all the events of the last five years. Suddenly people are aware of the lawsuit and its implications. The phone rings constantly. Many people had forgotten about the case, and most never knew why we sued the county in the first place.

The letters to the editor are the worst, because people don't actually have to confront us. Most of them have the same theme, "I think you're just out to make an easy buck with a frivolous lawsuit."

At choir practice one night, I stay after for snacks. I watch Linda across the room, wondering if we will ever be friends again. We've drifted apart these past few years, and I'm not sure I have the time or energy to work on the friendship. I'm eating some cheese and crackers and watching her when a new choir member comes up to me. He's middle-aged, a wine cooler in one hand, and doesn't even introduce himself.

"I don't understand how the county can be responsible in your lawsuit. After all, this is a wild animal that you're talking about."

I hate explaining the lawsuit to people who already have their mind made up. But I can't back away from him.

"Well, they should have warned us."

"Warned you? About a mountain lion that just wandered into the area? That's not their responsibility."

He's so abrasive. I'd rather just turn and walk away, but I explain.

"No, it isn't. But they knew that the mountain lion was a problem. As a matter of fact, there had been over thirty reported incidents in the three months leading up to Laura's attack. Most of them were just sightings of mountain lions, but some of them involved stalking by a lion, and one animal crouched down in front of a lady until the whole group threw stones and rocks at it till it ran away."

I can tell he's listening.

"The rangers kept a log of all the mountain lion incidents because they were worried about them. They started a policy that included honking the horn at mountain lions in campgrounds to get rid of them. They had conversations about what to do about the mountain lion. They even scheduled a meeting with the California Dept. of Fish and Game, the county, and the park, to decide what to do about the danger. The meeting was scheduled for two days after Laura was attacked."

"Oh, well, that's different. And they didn't warn you?" He backs off.

"No. They did warn some people, including a group of Boy Scouts the night before, but they didn't warn anyone going into the park on that Sunday."

"Oh, I didn't realize that. Well, good luck." He turns away.

By this time, a lot of people are listening and nodding their heads when I speak, but I'm tired of talking. I throw my paper plate in the trash and escape outside.

I think of all the conversations that start out with the person not understanding how we could sue the county, and end with people realizing that the county has been negligent. I'm tired of explaining.

When Mike came to the house and told us one thing at a time, or Rich called on the phone with another story, I tended to forget just how much evidence we had actually accumulated.

Only our closest friends understand what the case is all about and how complicated it is. If Wylie doesn't argue very well, and the county lawyers are as nasty as they were in the depositions, there's a huge chance that we'll lose.

Wylie's secretary calls the next morning and explains some of the trial procedure. Wylie wants us in the courtroom every day so that the jury can see us. Laura will come only when and if Wylie needs her to testify. He still hasn't decided.

I call my mom the next afternoon. "I don't know exactly when the trial will start, but I'm wondering if you can come out and be with the kids during the day."

She agrees to fly out. I think it'll be good for her now that Dad is gone, and I'll have a chance to see her and visit. I'd like the kids to get to know her better, since they haven't gotten that chance.

June 7, 1991

The trial is set to begin June 8, 1991, but we get a last minute phone call.

"This is Rich Cohn. Wylie wanted me to tell you that the trial's been postponed." The associate lawyer at Wylie's office just happens to be named Rich, just like our first attorney.

"Why?"

"The judge is going on vacation, and when he gets back Wylie will be on vacation. Also, the county now feels that the trial will take over twenty days."

"What difference does that make?"

"Well, Judge Firmat isn't supposed to hear cases that go over twenty court days, and the county feels that the case will be longer. If they can show why it will take longer, the judge will have to send it down to a different department."

My heart sinks. More waiting? Rich says that it could go to a retired judge, but Wylie is going to try to convince the judge that we can be finished in twenty days.

We might as well be on "People's Court." It seems like the case will never go to trial.

Wylie's secretary calls back the next morning and says that the trial is set for July 8, but no one's made a decision about who will hear it. It's useless to second-guess this system. The day I drive up to the courthouse is the day it will begin. I call Mom and ask her to wait.

Chapter 27

July 22, 1991

Don and I walk past the glass doors, into the seven-story Orange County Courthouse. The courthouse was modern in the fifties. Now the glass is held in place by rusted aluminum and the futuristic décor is old and dated. We buy a soft drink from the Middle-Eastern man at the newspaper stand and take the mirrored elevators up to the seventh floor. Plate glass windows line the right side of the long corridor. The courtrooms are to the left, behind plain wooden doors.

We find the courtroom that says "Francisco Firmat" and pull open the fake wood doors. A uniformed woman is standing at a desk, but the courtroom is empty as we slip into the faded theatre seats halfway back.

This is my first time in a real courtroom. It's a lot smaller than the ones on TV, and doesn't look as imposing and grand as I thought it would. The wooden jury box is over to the left; the witness stand is next to the judge's imposing bench. Along the other side, there are a few desks. In the center are two large tables, probably for the attorneys.

Wylie and Rich walk in with their oversized briefcases. I feel anxious now that we're down to the wire. We've heard for years about how good Wylie is supposed to be. People make him sound like a lawyer in a movie, but real life isn't like that.

Wylie certainly looks like he could be a star. Trim and sophisticated, with a silver glint in his hair, he exudes confidence and charm. He speaks well and I know he's very intelligent, but I don't think he's spent enough time with our case. He's left a lot of the work to Rich Cohn. Even though I hope not, I'm ready to be disappointed.

Barry Allen and two other defense lawyers set up at the other wooden table. The courtroom fills up quickly with the pool of potential jurors. I look behind me and there's standing room only. A reporter from the *Register* is sitting behind us doodling on a blank piece of paper. I recognize the reporter from the *Los Angeles Times*. The woman in uniform stands and comes smiling to the center of the courtroom.

"Superior Court, Department 22, Judge Francisco Firmat, is now in session. Please remain seated."

The judge, tall and stately in his black robes, strides in and nimbly climbs the two steps up to the bench. He has one streak of silver in his black hair, and looks like he's in his late forties. He nods to the lawyers, and begins to write. Rich comes over and whispers, "The bailiff says you'll have to wait out in the hall. We'll call you when there's room."

We nod and walk out through the throng of people waiting for jury duty. We find two folding chairs down the hall by the plate glass windows. Don goes to the cafeteria to get drinks. I feel out of place. The reporters and cameramen have also been thrown out of the courtroom to make room for the jurors. They sit around a table in the hall, laughing and getting comfortable, some reading the newspaper.

The summer heat covers Orange County like a grey shroud. The buildings shimmer in the heat, but it's cool inside the courthouse. I can't talk to the reporters. I'm not even supposed to look at the people waiting, in case one might end up on the jury. I sit quietly, staring out the windows, waiting for Don to get back.

He sits down next to me, hands me a Coke, and we wait silently.

"So what are you thinking about?"

He shrinks back in dismay.

I turn away from him, and take a sip of the sweet Coke. I think about all that's swirling through my head.

The trial is beginning. We can't be in the courtroom. I want to know what's happening in there. I hope the kids are ok with Mom at home. I wonder what they're doing. It's so hot and muggy today. I wonder how long the trial will last. I hope we win.

I wish I could talk to Don about all this, but it's hard. I need to talk and he doesn't. I take another sip of Coke and stare out the plate glass window. I wish I had brought a book.

The door to the courtroom opens and the jury pool files out for a morning break. Barry Allen waves away the reporters. Wylie smiles, looking fresh and confidant, and graciously answers the reporter's questions. They pile up in front of him, practically tripping over each other. I can hear some of his answers. Yes, he will put Laura on the witness stand, but he doesn't know when that will be. He sums up the major issues of the case in perfect sound bites.

I try to sink into my folding chair but he spots us down the hall and nods to us. The reporters turn on us as Wylie and Rich escape down the hall. We answer the same old questions with the same old answers. Yes, we're glad the trial is beginning. Yes, we would be willing to talk about a settlement, but the county isn't interested. We feel that the county was negligent in warning us about the dangers in the park. Yes, they had lion incidents before ours. And yes, I was right next to Laura when she was attacked.

The reporters gradually drift away after they have their fill, and Don and I go to lunch at a small café across the street. Over a tuna sandwich, Don starts to talk.

"I'm really annoyed with Wylie. I feel like we're being ignored."

"Yeah, I wish we had known before this morning that the trial would take six weeks. "

The judge announced that when we were first sitting in the courtroom.

Don goes on, "It's not so much Wylie, I guess. It's his office. They just forgot to call us and let us know."

"Yeah. I wish I had known that since Mom flew out here."

I take a bite of French fries dipped in ketchup.

"Wylie's working hard for us. I don't want to get annoyed at him."

"No, I'm not going to say anything."

Don grabs a few French fries off my plate. I push it over towards him to have more.

I put my greatest fear into words. "I sure hope he's as good as everybody says he is."

"Yeah, me too." Don finishes the last of his sandwich and we walk back to the courthouse. I'm surprised that Don talked as much as he did.

Late in the afternoon, Don and I finally get to go inside. There are twelve potential jurors sitting in the jury box. None of them look at us as we slip in the back. The judge is writing, and every few minutes he looks up. He seems to have no role in picking the jurors.

Wylie is at the podium, directing questions to the twelve jurors. But the other forty or fifty potential jurors in the courtroom have to listen to each question.

Wylie wants to know who has read the news accounts about Laura. One juror has just moved to Orange County, but most of them have heard of Laura and the mountain lion.

And then comes an important question, "Would you be able to put aside any opinions you have formed about this case, listen to the testimony, and judge this case solely on what you hear in this courtroom?"

Most of the jurors say yes, but one middle-aged Hispanic man raises his hand.

"Yes, sir?" Wylie looks at him and smiles.

"Well, I can't help but feel a lot of sympathy for that little girl. Everything that happened to her…"

Wylie answers with just the perfect amount of sympathy and justice thrown in. He says they wouldn't be human if each of them didn't feel sympathy for this poor little girl. But sympathy is not the issue in this case. Wylie pauses. The question is who is responsible for the extensive injuries to Laura, and does the man think he can put aside this sympathy and judge the case on the issue of responsibility?

The man hesitates a little too long before he answers and I'm guessing he'll be thrown off of the jury by the county. But it hardly matters. Wylie has been able to talk to the jurors about how good it is to have sympathy for Laura, and how that is what makes us human. He says that sympathy shouldn't influence their decisions, but I'm quite sure that Wylie hopes that all of them have an excess of compassion on which to base their legal decision. I know I do.

Each side has the right to dismiss up to eight jurors. It can be because of some obvious bias for either side, or, as Wylie says, "You might not like the color of their eyes."

Barry Allen asks the jurors about their camping experience, whether they had ever been to Casper's Park, what kind of wildlife groups they belong to, and if they've ever served on a civil case before. The questions finally stop for the day, to be continued in the morning.

The first juror to be dismissed by the county the next morning is an *LA Times* reporter. He had written an article about mountain lions a few years ago. He says he'd be fair but I'm sure he's anxious for a story. We dismiss a man who says that you assume risks when you go into a wilderness area.

The defense dismisses the Hispanic man. Wylie lets another man go for no apparent reason. I begin to wonder if we'll ever get a jury. The clerk picks more names at random to replace those dismissed, and the questions begin again. This time both attorneys shorten the process. The jurors have heard all the questions. If any of them have any reason to think they couldn't be impartial, they're required to say this now.

Both lawyers have to ask some questions to find out who the new people are and what they're thinking. A lot of people seem disappointed when they're dismissed. I wouldn't want to sit on a jury for six weeks, but a lot of people seem to want to.

It's late on Tuesday afternoon and I'm figuring we'll have another day of jury selection, when Wylie, sitting at the lawyer's table, suddenly says, "Your honor, I'm satisfied with the jury as is now stands."

After a few minutes of whispering with his other lawyers, Barry Allen agrees.

I watch as the jury leaves. A lot of retirees, a young student in her twenties, a business man with a phone in his hand. No one I know has a portable phone. I'm impressed and wonder how he can take six weeks off work. I heard he works at Disneyland. They all look like nice people. These are the people who will decide our case.

As Barry Allen gathers up his papers, I watch him closely. His face is flushed and unpleasant looking. I hate him, and I don't usually hate people. I know he's just doing his job. He needs to show that the county is not responsible for Laura's attack. But I sense something much deeper. I heard that he doesn't like Wylie and wants to get back at him for a case he lost to Wylie years before. I don't know if that's true, but he's certainly spent years preventing our case from ever coming to court. He's filed motion after motion, brought the case up to the Supreme Court of California where it was rejected, but delayed for another six months. He's questioned every injury of Laura's, all of which have been well documented. He's practically said that there is no reason for the lawsuit, implying that Laura's completely recovered.

Laura has recovered as much as possible from the attack. She will never regain the use of her right eye; her right arm and hand will always be paralyzed, and even though she can walk, she can't use her right foot to drive a car. She will always live in fear of aplastic anemia, never able to receive medical insurance. Although the scars have faded, the injuries are permanent.

I wonder if all defense lawyers disregard the truth, put the blame anywhere they can, and ignore human suffering. Our judicial system seems so intent on winning that it ignores the truth.

But Laura's suffering. That's what he won't see, and what I can't forgive him for not seeing. If the child lying there in intensive care that morning had been his child, I wonder what he would have thought.

Chapter 28

July 24, 1991

Most lawsuits are settled at the last minute, and I still have the tiniest hope that the county will want to settle. I don't know why, since in four years they've never shown any interest. No one calls, so Don and I drive to Santa Ana on a steaming July morning for the first day of the trial.

As we stand awkwardly in the corridor, I hear my name. I turn and see Greg Ysais, the man who drove off the mountain lion, walking towards us. How good he looks. His dark brown hair has grown to shoulder length, and he's tanned and slim. He approaches us with a new confidence and shakes our hands. It's pure joy to see him. Just as I'm feeling overwhelmed by the deception and posturing of the whole legal system, here is Greg. I can be as open and grateful as I want.

We'll listen to opening statements and Greg will be our first witness. My gratitude gets in the way of my ever really knowing him. He'll always be a hero to me. We've invited him to Christmas parties and he's come to a few, but we've never become friends. He always says, in his shy way, that anyone would have done the same. I don't believe that for a second.

Don opens the large wooden door. The jury is already seated and waiting. The courtroom is full, but we're able to find a few seats. The TV cameras are setting up and it's difficult to weave through the video equipment and cameras lining the back of the room. The judge comes in and Wylie stands up to give his opening statements. Wylie is all smiles and confidence. His suit and hair are immaculate, and he begins, speaking to the jury like he knows them all personally and is going to tell them a simple story.

The judge interrupts him after just a few minutes, saying he's very sorry but the cameras are too distracting and he's decided they should leave. The photographers and reporters can stay. It's the video cameras that have to go. They pack up their equipment and leave the courtroom quickly. It's much quieter after they leave.

Wylie begins again. He points us out in the courtroom, so the jury will see us and have our faces in their minds. He gives an overview of the whole case. He is persuasive; he is sincere; he makes you want to listen to his every word. He smiles; he knows when to add a touch of humor, and when to get serious again. He holds the jury in his hands. He is a master.

I'm prepared to be disappointed, but instead I'm overwhelmingly impressed. He's better than any lawyer I've ever seen in any movie. He is eloquent. He's able to do what I can't do— speak to a roomful of people and leave them hungry for more. My worries about Wylie not knowing the case disappear after a few minutes. He knows the case better than I do, and I was there. The jury is sitting at the edge of their seats as he sits down. I'm waiting for thunderous applause. I'm thrilled. And relieved.

Barry Allen is up next. He's a good speaker, and is clearly convinced that the county isn't responsible. But he's no Wylie. He seems angry; he doesn't smile; he gets flustered often. His thoughts don't connect as well as Wylie's, and he doesn't have the timing quite right. He gives a good opening statement, and if he had been up against an ordinary lawyer, he might have done an adequate job. But Wylie is a hard act to follow.

After the opening statements, we find Greg and go to a little coffee shop down the street. We talk about his divorce, our children, and all the time I watch him with a starry-eyed admiration. He's a real hero to me.

Greg isn't worried about being on the witness stand. All he has to do is tell the story he's told so many times before. There's nothing controversial about his testimony. He doesn't seem as shy as he used to be. I wonder what's happened. When we get back to the courthouse, Greg goes right up to the witness stand. It's strange listening to the whole story again from his unique viewpoint.

"Could you tell us what happened that Sunday, March 23, 1986, Mr. Ysais?"

"Well, my wife and daughter and I went to Casper's Park for a short hike. We were finished hiking and on our way back to the paved road when I heard what I thought were kids screaming. Then I listened closely, and I realized someone was in trouble. So I told my wife and daughter to stay where they were, and I ran toward the screaming. Then it stopped, and a boy ran up to me and pointed in the direction of the screams. I heard the screaming again and ran. I saw a woman, she was hysterical, and pointed toward a clump of cactus, and I jumped in and came face to face with a mountain lion."

"How big was the lion, Mr. Ysais?"

"It was about the size of a nineteen-year old man. It was huge. It had a baby by the neck and was snarling at me, and swiping at me with its paws while it held onto her.

I grabbed a branch and broke it off, and started poking the lion in the eyes. It kept swinging at me, but wouldn't let go of her. I kept getting in closer and trying to poke it in the eyes so it would let go. Finally it dropped her, and I got in between the baby and the lion, and said to the lady, 'Pick up your baby and get out of here.'

She grabbed her baby and then another man was there, so I ran back across the stream to get help."

I had never heard Greg tell the story in all the five years since the attack. He knew the lion was huge, too. I hadn't realized that.

I feel weak. The story still has power over me. There is so much I don't remember. I hear Wylie call David Pupkin to the stand. David and his girlfriend Jill had been the only other eyewitnesses to the attack.

When I had last seen David Pupkin, he looked like a hippie and spoke poor English. As he walks up to the witness stand, I don't recognize him. His hair is neat and he wears a suit right out of *GQ*. I'm even more surprised when Wylie starts questioning him. Instead of the hippie I remember, he is an extremely articulate person. He was born in South America, moved to Israel and is fluent in Hebrew, Danish, and now, English.

He and Jill had gone to the visitor's center that morning. They saw a small photo of a mountain lion as part of a wildlife display. Jill asked if there were mountain lions in the park. The ranger answered that there was a big one wandering in the park and they were trying to figure out what to do with it. Jill wanted to leave immediately, but David wanted to go for a short hike. The ranger assured them that mountain lions are afraid of humans.

They hiked by the stream and were sitting down to rest when they heard my screams. David ran toward the sound. He came up behind me and saw Laura in the mouth of the mountain lion. He yelled, "I'm going to get a gun." And he ran away to find some kind of weapon. He said that he had never been so terrified, even though he had been in the Israeli army for a few years.

As Greg and David Pupkin testify, the guilt that has grown inside of me all these years seems to shrink. These were both grown men, and they were terrified. Greg did something, but David ran away to get a gun. Maybe the fact that I was able to scream and not faint was the best I could manage.

I never felt guilt about the attack itself. I could never have prevented it.

What I felt guilty about was for doing nothing. That was the weight that I carried with me every day, that feeling of being inadequate, of not loving enough, of not being the person I wanted to be. I carried that horrible disappointment in myself all these years.

As I listen to Greg and then David, some of that weight seems to lighten. The guilt will be there forever, but it's a little less after today.

The next morning I get up early. Don's already reading the paper and I grab the front section to see the article about the trial.

"In opening statements, Wylie A. Aitken, the Small's attorney, said county officials knew about the danger of mountain lions but gave out brochures that stated 'the most dangerous wildlife in the park was poison oak.'

Aitken said that even after state authorities alerted the county to possible danger from mountain lions, county brochures said the cats 'had a healthy aversion to humans.' Aitken charged that the county had created part of the problem by luring wild animals into contact with humans by the way it positioned water troughs, shrubbery and eating places in the park.

County officials have denied any wrongdoing. The county's attorney, Barry Allen, told the jury that the county 'can't be liable for the acts of a wild mountain lion.'"

I hand the paper to Mom and give her a hug. Don calls to me from the living room, "We better leave now because of the traffic," and I run out the door for the second day of testimony.

The courtroom is crowded again. Everyone finally takes a seat, and the judge walks up to the bench. The first witness is a park ranger. He's a hostile witness, that is, someone who works for the county and should be testifying for them, but instead, is on our side.

The ranger's name is Darrell Bennett. He testifies that there had been several "unusual" mountain lion sightings at Caspers Wilderness Park in the months before Laura was attacked. At least twice before the attack on Laura, mountain lions had threatened hikers. On one occasion, a cougar charged at and circled two hikers, leaving only after they pelted it with rocks. Bennett was conducting a hike for ten children and four adults in November, when a mountain lion was spotted in a tree above the trail. He tried to scare it away with a branch, but it didn't budge.

The county had claimed in a brochure that "mountain lions were secretive and had a healthy aversion to humans."

"Did it seem secretive to you?" Wylie asked him.

"No."

"Did it seem to have a healthy aversion to humans?"

"No."

He said the lion appeared unconcerned by the hiker's presence and left only after he pelted it with broken twigs. After that and other incidents, Bennett's supervisor told him to consult state authorities. They said the sightings were "unusual" and advised that contact between the animals and the public should be avoided. Ironically, he noted, a meeting with state officials had been scheduled for the week following Laura's attack.

I watch the jury. They are listening intently. The next witness is a ranger named Bruce Buchman. He tells Wylie that there were unusual mountain lion sightings before Laura's attack. The cats seemed to be unafraid of humans and actually threatened them.

On March 4, a woman told rangers she was stalked by a lion. She and a friend watched the lion circle them and approach her in a crouch, as if ready to spring. It dashed up a tree after they pelted it with rocks. When Buchman went to investigate, he found the lion in the tree. It seemed unusually passive and calm in the presence of human beings.

"My concern was that a lion would approach a person on the trail. I became pretty concerned," Buchman testified.

On March 12, he went to his supervisor and discussed the possibility of posting warning signs throughout the park or verbally cautioning park visitors as they entered the area.

Buchman's supervisor said he would present the idea to the county's Risk Management Office for discussion. But before any decision was made, Laura was attacked. His testimony is particularly damaging because it shows that the county knew that the mountain lion was dangerous.

Four days before Laura was attacked, an aide to Orange County Supervisor Thomas Riley called him to ask about reports of aggressive mountain lions.

Wylie asked why he didn't warn visitors about the presence of lions, and Buchman replied that he first needed authorization from supervisors.

I've read the depositions of these witnesses and knew what they were going to say, but listening to their testimony is hard. The fear in their voices is different than reading about it in a deposition. One story after another shows how the strange and unusual mountain lion activity worried them. Worried them so much that they took action, reported their concerns, called the county, the state, and tried to do something. They were prevented by the inaction and bureaucracy of the county.

I hadn't realized how important these witnesses are for our case. And then Daryll Bennett says something that stuns me.

"I thought the county cared about people until the day after the attack. They told me to go and check the area where Laura was attacked. I wanted to take a gun, because the mountain lion was still in the area. The county official said 'No, we're not sending anyone with a gun out there. If Greg Ysais could scare off the lion with a stick, so can you.' That was it. That's when I realized that the county didn't care anything about the safety of people. I started speaking out about protecting the people coming to the park and was told to keep quiet."

Barry Allen tries to pick up the pieces with his cross-examination, but the testimony has been damning for the county.

Chapter 29

Don, Laura, and Susan in courtroom

Credit: Los Angeles Times

Monday, July 29

I'm trying to stay awake for the testimony about park management. The witness isn't very interesting, but he's necessary for Wylie's strategy. A large part of the testimony will show that the park is improved property and not a "wilderness" park. When we first started to hike there, it was called Casper's Regional Park. It was renamed Casper's Wilderness Park, probably to get more people to use the park. As it was renamed a "wilderness" park, it was actually being improved. The county built a visitor's center, improved the hiking trails, built stables and corrals for horses, and also designed a wonderful playground for children, which both our kids loved. We would hike, but we'd always visit the playground before we left.

The county says we should have known that a wilderness contained dangers, but we maintain that it wasn't a wilderness, except in name. It was an improved piece of property, especially where Laura was attacked. A lot of our witnesses testify about the improvements made to the park.

I want to bring Laura up to see the courtroom and hear the lawyers, but I don't want to let any reporters know she's coming. I also don't want her to hear the doctors. They should feel free to talk about her injuries and future disabilities.

We decide she can hear Mr. Spangenberg, the lawyer who was warned the night before Laura's attack.

Laura calls me into her room. "What do you think I should wear?" I'm glad to be consulted, so I help her choose a white skirt and top. I button the blouse for her, and then turn her around.

She looks older than ten. Her shoulder length brown hair is naturally curly. A few scars are still obvious on her face and her right eye is red and ugly. She has a large contact lens for that sightless eye that she has to put it in every morning. The contact covers her whole eye, and it looks just like her good eye. We went up to Los Angeles to get it made, by the same group that makes contacts for the movie industry. There's quite an art to making these. As I watched the woman spend hours trying to match the blue of Laura's eye, I never realized how many different colors go into making blue.

Laura doesn't look perfect, though. Her head looks terrible, because of the expanders, but she'll be wearing a hat.

Her right hand and arm are still barely functional. She hasn't moved her fingers since the day of the attack. She can hold things, but can't pick things up. A brace covers her right ankle, and she walks with a slight limp.

"Laura, you look beautiful." I give her a hug. She is beautiful, even after all she's gone through.

The next morning we bring Laura to court. The bailiff brings us up the elevator that the judges and employees use, so we can avoid the reporters.

"Stop!" Judge Firmat runs to the elevator and gets in. I don't know what to do, so I let him take the lead. He says "Hello" politely and then introduces us to another judge on the elevator. He jokes with the bailiff and a security guard, and luckily by then the elevator has stopped, so I don't have to think of what not to say next.

The bailiff shows Laura the courtroom and we have some cookies and coffee before the jury enters. One reporter spots Laura and pretty soon there's a cameraman and another reporter.

The first witness is David Spangenberg. I glance over at Laura, thinking she might be bored, but she sits quietly and seems to be interested.

Spangenberg and his disabled son visited the park on Saturday, where they met with other lawyers and their sons. The kids played all day in the hills above the campground, exploring and having fun. That night they went to a presentation where the ranger said to be careful of a "big male mountain lion that has come down into the park recently." He said they shouldn't run away from it, because it would attack. "It's better to just look large and yell at it, then throw rocks to drive it away."

Spangenburg and the other fathers are very upset that they weren't given this information when they came into the park, and they all decide to leave early the next morning, right before we come in.

At the recess, the bailiff helps Laura and me out the back door and down the elevator before the reporters see us.

After the recess we listen to a state biologist named Carl Wilcox. He was called just two weeks before Laura's attack by a ranger who detailed several unusual mountain lion sightings at the park. The ranger was concerned that the animal had boldly approached hikers. Wilcox recommended to the ranger to "warn park visitors and discourage human-lion contact." He also suggested that the lion be captured if it was spotted again.

Barry Allen gets Wilcox to admit that even though he thought the actions of the lion were "unusual," they did "not sound threatening." But Wilcox won't go any farther. He holds his ground and says, "Nonetheless, the cougar's behavior was odd enough to justify concern for the safety of park visitors."

Wylie has always said that Laura's attack was the result of negligence by county officials who knew there was a danger. The county has always denied this allegation. Wilcox's testimony shows that the county had been warned about the danger, not only from rangers but all the way up to state officials.

Barry Allen has said that nobody knew how dangerous mountain lions were because none had ever attacked a human in Southern California. He has said that the general belief was that mountain lions were shy, secretive and "had a healthy aversion to humans."

I'm a city girl and I didn't know much about mountain lions, although I've learned a lot in the last five years. But not admitting that mountain lions are dangerous always bothers me.

When I was young, I read the "Little House" books by Laura Ingalls Wilder. They were my favorite books and I even named Laura after the author. I practically had them memorized. There are stories in those books about mountain lions. One I especially remember was about Pa hearing the screams of a woman in the middle of the night. He goes on horseback with his rifle to the nearest neighbors, a few miles away. Their log cabin is quiet and dark. And then he hears the mountain lion scream close to him, and he rides home, shaking and worried the whole way. The next day he talks to an Indian chief and tells him about the lion. They go out together to shoot the lion because, as Pa explains to Laura, the Indian has children too, and he's very worried about the safety of his children.

That's not the only story in the book about mountain lions. They may be shy and you might never see one out in the wild, but they are dangerous. Pa knew that a hundred years ago. I can't get that story out of my mind, as the county continues to deny that obvious fact.

I'm glad we brought Laura up to the courtroom before she has to testify. She doesn't say much about the testimony she heard. She listened to it, but she's too young to understand the implications of Spangenberg's or Wilcox's testimony. When we get home, she's glad to go in her room and paint. She doesn't seem worried about testifying.

The next day I'm back in the courtroom alone. The judge asks Wylie for the next day's list of witnesses. Wylie says that he will call Maurice Hornekker, a mountain lion expert from Canada. The judge turns to Barry Allen, "And how long will the cross examination take?"

"A few days, your honor."

The judge frowns. I know he wants to keep the trial moving, but there's nothing he can do. Maurice Hornekker has published books and documentaries about mountain lions. He said in his deposition that the county should have known that the mountain lion is an opportunistic hunter that will attack small prey. I imagine that Barry Allen has spent a long time preparing for the cross-examination, even though I'm sure Hornekker will impress the jury with his extensive knowledge. Barry Allen probably should get him off the stand as soon as possible. Hornekker has studied cougars all his life.

Tuesday, July 30

In the morning I go to Wylie's office. Maurice Hornekker is in talking to Wylie. I meet him briefly. I've seen his documentary on mountain lions, and I'm anxious to hear his testimony. Wylie and I walk to the courthouse. Hornekker doesn't need to be in the courtroom until the first witness is finished, so he waits in Wylie's office. Someone will bring him to the courthouse when they're ready for his testimony.

Barry Allen finishes up cross-examining a witness, and then Wylie stands up, puts his hands on the podium, and calls a completely different witness to the stand. He's skipping Maurice. I look up in surprise.

Barry Allen's face turns beefy red. He looks furious. He's prepared for days to cross-examine Hornekker and now a witness is being called for whom he isn't the slightest bit prepared. Barry Allen stomps up to the bench. Wylie follows with a slightly bemused, innocent smile, like he can't imagine what could possibly be wrong. I'm sitting close enough that I can hear them.

"Your honor," Barry Allen spits out the words, "Mr. Aitken never intended to call this witness. He's not even here in California. Your honor, Mr. Aitken lied about calling this witness to the stand. He made the defense prepare for this witness and he's not even in this country." The veins bulge out in his neck. I wonder idly if he'll have a heart attack.

Wylie smiles, "Your honor, I don't think that the jury needs to hear two days of cross-examination of this witness. I fully intended to have Maurice Hornekker take the stand. I just now made up my mind that it's not necessary, mostly because of the lengthy cross, your honor. As to the witness not being here, I'll be glad to send for him. He arrived from Toronto last night and is prepared to testify for the next two days. He's in my office as we speak. I can send for him right now…" He motions to Rich Cohn, who starts to stand.

The judge looks at Barry Allen, who mutters something I can't quite hear. Then he sits down and glares as Wylie smiles at the next witness. Did Wylie deliberately lie about the witness and fly him down from Toronto knowing full well that he wouldn't be using him? I don't know. I do know that Hornekker is in Wylie's office because I saw him. And I'm sure Wylie doesn't want his witness cross-examined for two whole days. Whatever the truth is, Barry Allen looks furious.

At the lunch break, we don't even talk about Hornekker. Wylie tells us that he's decided not to show the pictures of Laura taken in the emergency room right after the attack.

"What do you mean, not show them to the jury? They need to know how terrible her injuries were." I can't believe that he wouldn't show the jury those pictures. We need the jury to see how badly she was injured.

Wylie explains. "It's a very fine line between sympathy for Laura and photos that are too horrible for the jury. I don't want them disgusted or repulsed by the photos. It might have the opposite effect from what we want."

I'm furious. "But they need to know. They need to see how bad her injuries were."

"Trust me on this one. I think it's better that we don't show the worst photos. The jury will get the picture."

So in the end we trust Wylie, and Dr. Watanabe shows a few photos, but not the ones taken the day of the attack. I keep my copies of the pictures in a box out in the garage. Maybe when Laura is an adult she'll want to see them.

Dr. Palmer, Dr. Weiss, and Dr. Shannon are all called to testify. There are no surprises. Their testimonies are very technical and the cross-examinations are short. I realize again as I listen to them, how lucky we were to have a trauma hospital close by, staffed with a superb team of doctors.

Chapter 30

Sue's testimony

Credit: Los Angeles Times

August 4

I sit up in the choir loft on the weekend, noticing how the fans blow the hanging microphones ever so slightly, creating tiny shadows that move against the pale green walls. I look past the microphones to the stained glass windows. I'm trying not to listen to Father

Sam, a visiting priest. He's come to do a retreat, and the church is packed. I'm hired to play one song at the beginning and one at the end. His next sentence catches my attention.

"One Holy Week when I was on retreat. I thought a lot about the sufferings and death of Jesus. I could feel his pain, and imagine what it was like for him, and what he suffered. It was the worst week of my life."

I look away from the windows, not believing what I just heard. If that was the worst week of his life, then I should be up there talking and he should be out in the congregation listening to me. I think of all the people in the church, elderly women who have lost a husband or perhaps a child. Some don't have a job, or are in danger of losing their home. There are parishioners sitting in front of him who have debilitating mental and physical illnesses. I notice a few in wheelchairs, people in constant pain every day of their life.

And Father Sam's worst week was when he *thought* about Jesus' suffering? I think about the many sermons I've heard over the years. During my whole childhood, and every day in the convent, I listened to so many endless sermons by priests who hadn't experienced even the basics of life.

They've told me when to feel guilty, how to worship God, not to use birth control, how to raise my children, and to pray for my atheist husband. They've even told me how to have a happy marriage. The more I think about it, the angrier I get. Why have I listened to someone else tell me how to live my life all these years? I know most of these priests. They're not any smarter than I am, they don't know much about God, and they certainly don't know anything about relationships.

From this moment on, I vow, I will only listen to people who are experts, who have put a lifetime into whatever they do best. Otherwise, it's like learning piano from someone who's never played.

But I'm most angry with myself, for listening all these years.

I'm so busy being angry, I almost miss the final hymn. I slide onto the organ bench, play, and take a last look at the choir loft before I leave. How I wish I could leave and never come back. But playing for the church is what I know and do best. It's the perfect job, except for that one tiny problem of not believing in God.

August 6, 1991

On Monday morning Don and I are back in the courtroom. I know that Barry Allen will ask me about the pamphlet. He's already brought it up in my deposition. He asked if "I really believed that poison oak was the most dangerous thing in the park", and I answered, "Yes."

Barry Allen says that the pamphlet was just worded that way to be cute and appealing, not to make people give up their responsibility to think. But the truth is pretty simple. I never dreamed that there could be a mountain lion in the park, especially so close to our home in Orange County. I believed the pamphlet.

The reason the pamphlet is so important is because the county is not obligated to warn us about dangers, according to the law. But as Mike explained it many times over the last few years, "If they know of a danger and do or say nothing, they're fine. If they know of a danger, but deliberately and knowingly tell us there is NO danger, then they're legally responsible."

"So that pamphlet is really important."

"You bet it's important. It's probably the most important piece of evidence that we have. And the fact that you saw it and relied on it is equally important."

My testimony is scheduled for tomorrow. I'm listening to one of our witnesses, but more worried about being up on the witness stand. I'm terrible at public speaking, and have avoided it all my life. I wish I could be like Wylie, confident and flawless, but I'm not. There's a part of me that wants to tell what really happened. I've been accused of leaving Laura alone in the park, and I want to make it clear that I was there with her. Finally everyone has to listen to me. I have nothing to hide. No drugs, no alcohol, no negligence, no arguments about custody, no deceit, and no lies.

August 7, 1991

The next morning, Wylie calls me to the witness stand. I walk up to the small box. Everyone is looking at me. My mouth feels like cotton. I can't swallow. I promise to tell the truth. The courtroom looks bigger from the witness stand and there are reporters lining the back wall. Don is out there, but I can't find him. I glance at the judge. He's looking at Wylie, and I follow his glance. Wylie smiles and walks up to the witness stand, looking over the top of his glasses.

"Mrs. Small, could you tell us what happened on March 23, 1986?" As I start to speak, the fear slips away.

After I finish answering a few questions, Wylie asks me to come down and help explain a videotape of Laura. The video contains pieces of family and hospital videos that he has put together from the past five years.

I try to explain what it's been like to see Laura suffer, not only during the months in the hospital, but through all the eye operations and the aplastic anemia. I want to cry, but I don't let myself. The time on the witness stand slips by quickly, and suddenly we're finished. Wylie thanks me and sits down.

Barry Allen picks up a few papers, walks to the witness stand, and smiles at the jury.

"Is Laura in a special class at school?"

"Yes, she's in a GATE program." We have nothing to hide. Let him ask. I try to conceal my dislike of Barry Allen. I think about Wylie and how he always smiles.

"Did you look at the pamphlet about Casper's Park at any time after Laura was attacked?'

"After she was attacked?" I'm confused. Why would I look at the pamphlet right after the attack? And why is he asking that question?

"Yes. You might have seen it on the floor of the car and picked it up."

I think for a minute, not understanding.

"Well, no, I don't think so. Laura was in intensive care. I didn't read anything then." And suddenly I realize what he's doing.

275

He wants to suggest that I read the pamphlet not before, but after Laura's attack. He's implying I had picked up the pamphlet afterwards looking for evidence against the county. I breathe a sigh of relief.

"Do you think that Laura is smart?"

I hate this man. If I answer yes, then Laura's recovered and we have no case against the county. If I say she isn't, then I betray my daughter and my love for her.

"Yes, I think she's smart." And I think she's beautiful and kind and caring and everything I could ever want in a daughter. I want to add all that, but I don't.

"No more questions, your honor."

That was it! I'm shocked as I stand up. I expected the cross examination to be longer. The judge calls for a recess and I go back to the jury room to get Laura. She's ready and the cameras are set up. I sit weakly next to Don who takes my hand.

"You did great!" he whispers.

Laura has to raise her right hand, not her left. She lifts it up with obvious difficulty, and it's an awkward motion. Her paralysis is obvious.

Wylie leans over her and says something. She and Wylie smile at each other; he's turned slightly facing the courtroom, and I see the flashing of all the cameras in the back of the room. I have a feeling the picture will be in the newspaper. I wonder if Wylie planned to do that. Then I realize, of course he did.

My hands are tightly clenched as Wylie starts the questioning. I hope that she'll do ok and not get confused or upset. She's only ten years old.

"Laura, do you fight with your brother?"

Laura looks momentarily confused.

"No."

"Remember, Laura, you're under oath to tell the truth."

Everyone in the courtroom laughs, including Laura. Wylie has put her at ease with just one question, and I breathe easier.

Wylie asks her about the day of the attack. She remembers bits and pieces of it. Then they talk about problems Laura has had since the attack.

Laura doesn't even remember seeing from both eyes. And all the new skills she's learned since age five, like tying her shoes, opening a can, or cutting up food; she's learned to do all of them one-handed.

Laura talks about the ridicule and meanness of her fellow classmates in school. It's hard to hear about all of this from Laura's viewpoint. I realize that there was a lot she hasn't told me.

After about fifteen minutes, although it seems like an eternity, Wylie thanks her and walks back to his desk smiling.

With a sharp screech on the floor, Barry Allen pushes his chair back and stands up with his yellow legal pad. He walks quickly to the podium. I wonder if he's going to try to confuse her, or ask difficult questions. I think he'd be wise to get her off the witness stand quickly.

He asks her what activities she likes, how she's doing in school, and he's getting the answers that he wants. The county has waited till most of her injuries are healed, and they want the jury to see a perfectly normal ten-year old.

Laura had asked me at the beginning of the summer if she could do some chores, like cleaning and laundry, for some extra money. And since my mom came out, Laura's been helping with the cooking. Every day when Don and I get home, there's a meal ready for us.

Barry Allen asks his next question.

"What have you been doing this summer?"

Laura looks right at him. "Cleaning and laundry."

Barry Allen glares at her. "That's what you've been doing this summer?"

That's certainly not the answer he wanted. I'll bet he wanted a list of swimming, having fun at the mall, playing video games, anything that would paint her as totally normal, totally recovered.

"Yes."

I can't laugh out loud, but I'm laughing inside.

Barry Allen looks down at his yellow legal pad. "No more questions, your honor."

He glares at me for a second, like it's my fault, then walks to his desk and throws the yellow pad down angrily.

I motion to Wylie, and he comes over to me.

"Ask her why she's been cleaning and doing laundry."

Wylie smiles and walks up to the witness stand. "Tell me about this cleaning and laundry."

Laura is eager to tell him. "Well, my grandma came out from St. Louis to be with us during the trial, so I'm helping her. She really likes to clean—a lot! And I'm doing the laundry so I can make extra money to spend for things I want to buy, like CD's and stuff."

Wylie smiles knowingly and turns slightly to the jury. "We all know how grandmothers can be."

Most of the jury members are smiling.

Don testifies next. He breaks down and cries during part of the testimony, which surprises me. He's so good at holding his emotions inside, and now, in front of everyone, he gets very emotional. But it means a lot, to see a man who is obviously so intelligent and controlled, to become so upset over his daughter's injuries.

As he steps down from the witness stand, I'm so proud of him. For all he's done. For all the time he's given to Laura's recovery, and his tireless work to keep us all going financially and emotionally.

And so we rest our case. The picture of Laura and Wylie is on the front pages of the *Los Angeles Times* and the *Register* the next morning. Wylie might have planned the photo, but he couldn't plan how nice it looked. I'm so proud of Laura.

Wylie doesn't seem at all concerned about the county's defense, but then, I've never seen Wylie worried about anything. Rich takes me aside. "Don't worry, Wylie is the best cross-examiner I've ever seen."

Chapter 31

Laura on witness stand

Credit: Los Angeles Times

The following Monday the defense begins their portion of the trial. Barry Allen parades a lot of county employees on the witness stand. The verses are slightly different, but the refrain is the same.

"Yes, I knew it was a dangerous situation, and that's why I called, wrote, or talked to someone. I was worried but no one did anything."

Everyone says they knew something was wrong and tried to warn the public. I can't tell if they're all lying or they really did try. Probably the truth is somewhere in between.

Most of the witnesses don't seem to be helping the county, because they're saying that the park was dangerous, and they all tried to do something about it.

Wylie can't bring up the Mellon case, because it happened after Laura's attack. But he'd love to show the jury the picture that was taken the day before Justin's attack-the one that shows the mountain lion in the grass behind the couple with the baby. Wylie slides the 16x20 poster in a large manila envelope and keeps it next to his table in the courtroom, hoping to get an opportunity. He can only show it if the county brings up Justin's attack, and that's not very likely.

August 13

Paul Beier, another expert witness for the county, is being cross-examined by Wylie.

"What are your credentials, Mr. Beier?"

"I've read a lot of books about mountain lions."

Wylie looks at him, and moves his wire rimmed glasses down a bit to see him better.

"How many books have you read?"

Paul Beier looks up at Wylie.

"All of them."

Wylie strides back to the desk, takes off his glasses and holds them, letting the jury think about that answer.

Wylie asks more questions, and Beier finally says, "What happened to Laura is a once in a lifetime event. No one can foresee a mountain lion attack. If a mountain lion is in a certain vicinity, then the next day the mountain lion will be twenty miles away."

"Are you sure of that, Mr. Beier."

"Yes, I am."

If this is true, and the jury believes him, then the county would have no reason to warn anyone. If mountain lions cover a large area at random, then the county would never know there was one in the area.

"Your honor, may I approach the bench?" Wylie asks in his gravelly voice.

The judge nods.

I have no idea what's happening.

"Your honor, the time has come. I have that photo and can impeach this witness. It was taken a day before a second mountain lion attack and fits my argument that the county had a duty to warn the Small family there was an element of risk in taking a hike in Casper's Park. Either the witness is sadly mistaken or else he is deliberately misleading the jury and that's for the jury to decide."

The judge turns to Barry Allen.

"You opened the door." The judge nods to Wylie.

Now I understand. This is about the photo of the lion in the grass.

Wylie picks up the manila envelope. He slowly takes out the picture and turns to the jury, holding it up so they can see it clearly. They stare at the photo, not seeing anything but the happy family and the tall grass behind them. Then as Wylie points out the lion, I can see the sudden change in their faces to fear and then to the realization that Paul Beier had just been proven wrong, without a doubt. The picture of the lion is put on the exhibit table in front of the courtroom and Wylie has no more questions for the witness.

At the dinner table that night we all laugh about Beier's credentials and how some people can reach high positions by sheer luck. I've read a lot of books about mountain lions since the attack, but I've never claimed to be an expert.

The next day, Barry Allen calls Mr. Riley, a county supervisor, to the stand. Allen asks if the county thought there was any risk of a mountain lion attack. Of course, they never dreamed it was possible. Then Allen asks why the county didn't put up a sign to warn people about the non-existent threat.

Mr. Riley smiles. He talks about how complicated this is, and how it normally takes six months to get a sign made to warn people.

"You have to put in a request, then it has to be reviewed, it has to be approved. After that, the sign has to be designed with the correct wording, then the order has to go through. It then is sent to a graphics lab. When it's finished, it has to be installed. The whole process is complicated and can take up to six months."

I'm smiling as I think about Wylie cross-examining him.

Wylie walks to the jury box. He talks about all the ways people can warn others of a danger, like he's thinking out loud about this for the very first time. The jury listens to every word. The county could have closed the park, they could have closed the trail, they could have put up a hand-written sign, or posters that had been xeroxed, or they could have warned people verbally. All these things could have been done before six months had gone by. I notice quite a few jury members nodding in agreement.

Mr. Riley repositions himself in the witness chair, looking uncomfortable.

"Were you at the park after Laura Small was attacked?"

"Yes, I went down to the park the day after the attack. I hiked out to the area by the stream, but the water in the stream was so high that I couldn't cross it, and I was unable to see the site of the attack."

I almost laugh out loud. I had already told the jury that we had waded through the stream and stood ankle-deep looking for tadpoles.

Wylie asks the supervisor if he felt that the stream was dangerous, being so high, and Riley answers, "Yes."

Wylie walks to his desk and shuffles a few papers. He turns to Riley and quotes my testimony about the stream being only a few inches high, and mentions that Laura was wading in the stream when she was attacked. Wylie asks him again if the stream was too dangerous to cross.

"Yes."

"No more questions, your honor."

The next witness manned the entrance booth at the park that Sunday. Wylie asks him if he knows anything about parks and wildlife. He says he knows nothing. He just collects the money at the entrance booth.

Then he volunteers a statement before Wylie asks anything. He says, robot-like, "I warned all the people who came into the park that Sunday that there were dangerous mountain lions in the park."

Wylie mentions that Don and I didn't get a warning from him. He shrugs his shoulders and repeats, "I warned everyone that there were dangerous mountain lions in the park."

Wylie asks if he warned Greg Ysais and his family.

"I warned everyone that there were dangerous mountain lions in the park."

"Mr. Ysais told us in this courtroom that he was not warned when he went into the park that Sunday."

The man stares blankly ahead.

"I warned everyone that there were dangerous mountain lions in the park."

Wylie lists all the people who have already testified that they weren't warned, and with each he answers with the same robotic statement. I'm almost laughing out loud and I can see curious smiles on the faces of the jury. I've never heard anyone give the same answer more than a dozen times, with no change of expression. I wonder if there's something seriously wrong with him, or perhaps he was told by the county to give only that answer.

Wylie's last question has to do with the witness's current employment.

"Where are you working now?"

"I'm not working at Casper's Park any more. I was promoted."

"No further questions, your honor."

Wylie walks back to the table. Another successful day.

Chapter 32

August 18, 1991

It amazes me how quickly my belief in God has collapsed. It took four years to get to that moment, but once I was there, my faith crumbled to dust. It's as if I stood out in the audience all these years, watching the play, and now I'm backstage and see that all those beautiful buildings and decorations are just props, made out of paper mache and held up by a few flimsy boards and nails.

During sleepless nights worrying about the trial, I also deconstruct my once-solid faith, finding out there is nothing to it. I try to discover one strong piece of evidence that will convince me of its truth or stability, but all of them crumble at my touch.

I think about the host at the Benediction service. Catholics believe that this host IS God, that the priest turns this simple piece of bread into the body and blood of Jesus. Why would the creator of the universe transform himself into a tiny piece of bread so that ten bored people at Benediction can worship him? When I think about it, I don't know whether to laugh or cry. The very thought is ridiculous.

I think about God's great eternal plan. It includes millions of embryos that aren't born because of spontaneous abortions, millions of infants and children dying before the age of one from Aids or starvation. It's a horrible plan, one that would come from an impersonal universe rather than a loving, caring God.

Original sin, one of the great tenets of Christianity, seems cruel and vindictive. We are never allowed to blame the child for the sins of the parent, and yet that's exactly what God has done for untold generations.

And Christ had to come to earth and be killed to make up for the mistake that Adam and Eve, mythical figures at best, had made in the dawn of history. What a bizarre idea this was, when I backed up and took a look at it objectively.

If I were God, and some random person I had created made a mistake, I wouldn't blame every single person on earth, and then kill my son to make up for it. But that's what original sin is, in the definition of the church.

Every belief collapsed one by one. Instead of regretting my decision on that night of the Vigil, I begin to wonder why it took so long.

August 19

The next day the defense calls a witness from the California Department of Fish and Game. He's dressed in his brown ranger uniform and badge, and strides confidently to the witness stand. He was one of the officials who had been invited to the Tuesday meeting. Wylie reads a quote from his deposition where he says that mountain lions are "not dangerous." The witness agrees he made the statement. I have a feeling that this is going to be another great day for us. Wylie asks the official to describe a situation in which a mountain lion could be considered dangerous.

"I can't think of any."

Wylie stops as he's walking to his desk. He turns toward the witness stand and adjusts his glasses.

Seated about halfway back in the courtroom, I cringe and wait for the show to start. I actually feel sorry for the man, because I know what's going to happen and the poor man doesn't. No one can say something like that to Wylie and get out of the courtroom alive. Talk about a dangerous situation!

Wylie walks to the witness stand slowly, and describes a situation out in the wilderness where a lion has been seen.

"Not dangerous."

Then the lion comes closer, and has been seen in the campgrounds during the day.

"Not dangerous."

Now the mountain lion approaches the campers at a campfire.

"Not dangerous."

Now Wylie talks about a little child at the campfire.

"Not dangerous."

Now Wylie goes in for the kill. I'm smiling.

"Ok, there's a small child alone in a room with a mountain lion. Would you describe that as a dangerous situation?"

The ranger shrinks back in the chair. He's gone this far, and he knows that Wylie will pounce if he says the situation is dangerous. He would impeach himself, because he's already stated that there isn't a situation in which a mountain lion is dangerous.

He whispers, "No, I don't think it would be dangerous."

I can hear the gasps of the jury.

"So a small child in a living room alone with a mountain lion wouldn't be dangerous? Please speak up so the jury can hear you."

"No, I don't think it would be dangerous."

"No further questions, your honor."

The man stands up, looks down at the floor, and makes his way quickly out of the courtroom, not looking at anyone. Wylie walks back to the table.

August 28, 1991

The trial lumbers on endlessly. My initial worries about Wylie have been swept away by his brilliant displays in the courtroom, especially his ability to cross-examine the defense witnesses. A random remark in a deposition is all Wylie needs. He carries it to its logical conclusion, destroys whatever point the witness was making, and leaves them wondering what happened.

The defense wraps up its testimony and the closing arguments are presented. Wylie's argument is persuasive and eloquent. The jury goes out to deliberate. Don and I sit outside in the corridor waiting and talking about the trial. No one knows how long the deliberations will take.

If the lawsuit were to be decided on the merits of the lawyers, we would win. But there is a lot of uncertainty in the law. The mountain lion had wandered into Casper's Park. The park was called a wilderness area, even though we tried to prove it was developed. And we were the underdogs, one family against Orange County. I had watched the jury all during the trial, but I could never tell what they were thinking.

If we win the lawsuit, I'll be very pleased with the person I'll be. I imagine saying to the reporters, "Well, the money was never the important thing. It's the fact that Laura is alive and doing so well, and that we've all managed to survive the difficult times."

I can almost taste the words in my mouth, knowing where my priorities are and always have been, that life and happiness are more important than money.

It's losing that I worry about. I don't know that part of myself nearly as well. I'll have to deal with sudden depression, and the unfairness of it all. I'll try to convince myself that we're somehow better off losing, but I'm going to be angry with the county, the lawyers, and the whole legal system.

I know I can be mean and petty. I want revenge against the people who hurt Laura. I want the money for her, to make up for all that has been taken from her. If we lose, I'll be furious. And I won't have a clue how to deal with these feelings, because in all these years I've never really listened to them.

The jury sends out a single question. They need the definition of "improved property." I shake my head in despair. If they missed that major part of Wylie's argument, that Caspers was improved property, and NOT a wilderness area, then we've lost for sure. Wylie sends back the definition, and I wonder if he's thinking the same thing, that the jury just isn't getting it. But he continues to be his usual confident self.

That evening, after everyone's gone to sleep, I pick up an old *Reader's Digest*. I thumb through an article about a family's medical trauma. They always have the same predictable stories: a beautiful story of family, love of God, and teaching others to be grateful. The wife is now a motivational speaker and gives lectures all over the country.

I put the magazine down. I'm so disappointed in myself. I used to believe in God; now I believe in nothing. We used to have the time to enjoy our family. Now Don and I struggle to talk to each other. The couple in the story got closer and relied on their love to get them through their experience. Don and I have drifted apart. I don't want to burden him with my feelings. Our marriage has stayed intact, but we really don't talk much.

What would I say as a motivational speaker? I've learned nothing. Five years have gone by since the attack. I could have gotten a Ph.D, given concerts, or started a new career. It's so depressing to go through all this, only to learn nothing and have done nothing. What a waste. I'm not even a better person. I lock up the house and climb into bed quietly so I don't wake Don. I feel so close to tears.

It takes me a long time to fall asleep. I toss and turn. Now I'm in a long dark corridor with wooden doors up ahead of me. I must be in the convent. Huge cathedral doors stretch upward, ornately carved. I pull on the rusted iron handle, and light streams past me, filling the corridor. As my eyes adjust to the brightness, I step slowly into a garden. Glass is above me and on all sides, held together with scrolled rusted ironwork. I've stepped into a garden of such beauty that I almost forget to breathe. Climbing up the towering glass walls are morning glories and bougainvillea, the delicate red and blue flowers intertwined. The vines stretch across the high ceiling, held by some magic.

I walk slowly down worn stone steps. Trumpet trees with their pale pink flowers line a flagstone pathway. Green moss grows in between the stones. Soft velvet roses, red and yellow, dot the green like an artist's palette. Irises tower behind the roses, their purple softness crowned with yellow. I come to an old wooden bridge across a stream. I'm almost to the back wall of the garden. Now I hear birds in the trees and watch them flit from branch to branch, darting high to the ceiling and back again. I hear a whirring and turn to see a hummingbird staring at me, its ruby throat shimmering in the light, before disappearing in a flash.

I sit in a wrought iron chair and soak in the beauty around me. The path is wet. I wonder if there are vegetables. And sure enough, by the left wall, are rows of corn. I get up and wander further down another path. The squash would be over by the gate and the sunflowers are by the wall, where I always plant them. And the tomatoes should be down further. I remember more and more as I step along the path. If I walk a little more I'll see them. They're huge and red, dripping from the plants like Christmas ornaments.

This is my garden, the one I planted long ago. I've forgotten about it. I thought it had died. But it's been growing, secretly, all this time. It's been growing, without my even knowing. I haven't taken care of it. I haven't watered it. But it's beautiful. It all belongs to me. The prosaic vegetables, the poetry of the flowers, their colors intermingled like a Monet painting. The light is mine, streaming through the glass high above. This is my garden. This garden is me. I hear soft music from the alarm clock. The white popcorn ceiling of my bedroom gradually appears above me. I see the light stream through the blinds. It was only a dream.

I smile. I know for certain, without a moment's thought, without a question, what the dream means. The garden in my dreams is me—my deepest self. And everything that's happened in my life since the accident. My family, the constant questions, the sacrifices for Laura— all this hasn't been worthless. It's been growing there, silently, all this time. I get up slowly. I want to live in the dream.

I think about the dream often that day, even though I'm at the courthouse. The dream opens my eyes to all I have been missing. Our family is good and whole, and Don and I, though we have our troubles, are still together. David and Laura are beautiful children and I couldn't be more proud of them.

Instead of a vast emptiness where God used to be, there is a garden. A garden of caring, of love, and of friendship. I could be that motivational speaker. I'm not going to talk about God any more, but I have found something these last five years. My eyes open to the garden growing inside me that I had missed.

Chapter 33

August 30, 1991

I decide to bring Laura to the courthouse with me, even though there isn't much to do there. I know my mom is tired of babysitting, although she would never say that. The jury has been deliberating for two days. Don has to work, so I'll come every day for as long as it takes. Laura and I sit in the hall while the jurors walk by. I try not to look at them. The smell of old sweat and perfume fills the hall and I wish for a fresh breeze.

At nine o'clock we walk into the courtroom and sit close to the front. I feel people staring at us. Judge Firmat sends the jury out for deliberation. That's it. We made our appearance for the day and now we wait. Wylie walks up to us with a big smile on his face. He's a good actor. I don't feel like smiling.

"Let's go back to my office. You can wait there. These things can take a long time."

We sit in the Wylie's law library for most of the morning, reading the "Neverending Story." I have a hard time concentrating. Wylie's office is cool in the summer heat and I wish for a moment that I had studied the law contained in those massive law books that line the room. Instead, I come up with an idea to keep both of us entertained. "Let's tell a story. I'll start and then you make up the next part and we'll just keep going back and forth."

We make up a story that gets crazier each time till it falls apart into complete nonsense. Wylie comes to the door as we're laughing.

"Are you ready to go back?"

We walk over for our midday appearance. I'm sweating, but Laura looks cool in the heat. Wylie thinks it's important that we're there in front of the jury when they go in and out, just to remind them that the case is about Laura and her future.

The reporters sit down the hall as we wait. I look out the plate glass windows to the haze below us. The only summer I know this year is the one in the courtroom, where the air conditioning dictates the highs and lows for the day.

The jury walks out quickly, anxious to eat lunch. Some of the younger ones run to the elevator. All I want is one glance, one look from one of them to show they're on our side, but none of them looks at us. Wylie is down the hall, talking to another lawyer.

Rich comes up to Laura and me, ignoring the cameramen and reporters.

He leans over and whispers, "They've reached a verdict, but don't let anyone know. The judge doesn't even know yet. The bailiff just told me."

My stomach turns over and knots even tighter than before. Rich and Laura and I walk down the hall to the elevator.

"I'll tell Wylie."

"I'll go to the office and call Don."

I dial Don's work number, my fingers shaking. The Musak sounds tinny in my ear as I wait.

"They've reached a verdict. You can make it since they won't be back till 1:30."

"Ok, I'll be there."

I debate whether to call my mom. No, there's no reason to worry her even more. It won't be much longer.

"Laura, let's go have lunch at the Boardwalk café." I walk, holding Laura's hand, as she practically dances down the sidewalk, her brown curls bouncing under her straw hat.

She looks up at me. "Don't worry, if we don't win, so what? We'll be fine, no matter what they decide."

I've said those words to Laura for the last five years. I know they're true. We will be fine. Laura's made a remarkable recovery and we have a beautiful family. I know it's true.

But just now, knowing that we could lose, I'm filled with apprehension about the future. I'll be angry, devastated, and bitter. I can't think of all the words that'll describe how horrible I'll feel. We've gotten by without the county's help. But why does Laura have to suffer any more from their mistake? I can't stop thinking about it.

Laura and I sit down in the restaurant with all the lawyers and judges. The older blonde waitress knows us by now. "How's it going?"

"Ok. Still not over."

"Well, I hope you win," she says loudly to everyone as she walks back to the counter.

"So do I," I whisper to Laura.

Laura and I split a tuna sandwich, but I push my half over to her. I'm sure it's good, but nothing looks very appetizing right now.

"Mom, you really should eat something. Have a French fry."

I try one, but it tastes like straw with ketchup.

"Hurry up sweetie, we'd better get back. Maybe dad's there."

"Mom, we just got here."

"I'm a nervous wreck."

"Oh really?"

We pay our bill and hurry back to Wylie's office, which is humming with activity. I see Don and slip my hand into his. He's nervous too, trying to look confident. His face is tight and he can't seem to smile.

"Good luck. We know you'll do great. Don't worry." Wylie always represents big cases, but this one has even more publicity than most.

We walk to the courthouse together. Wylie is smiling, but Rich looks worried. The reporters are waiting outside the courtroom. The bailiff unlocks the door. The cameras are set up and take pictures of us sitting there. People are waiting outside. There's not enough room for everyone. I feel like a dishrag. Wylie is smiling and talking to Rich, like it's an ordinary moment.

I sputter nonsense to Laura, just to keep talking so we don't have to sit in this oppressing silence, with the cameras on us.

"The jury will come in and the foreman will hand the verdict to the judge. If he says 'in favor of the plaintiff', then that means we win. If he says 'in favor of the defense', that means we lose? Ok?" I know this because I've seen it in movies.

"Mom, you already told me that," Laura reminds me. She's wearing a pink and blue flowered dress with a straw hat to cover up her swollen head. She looks fresh and beautiful in the summer heat.

The clock on the wall clicks loudly and the hand jumps to 1:30. The jury has already come back into the jury room. We wait for another five minutes. Apparently one of the jurors is late getting back from lunch. The minutes tick by.

Wylie, smiling confidently and looking camera-ready in his gray pin-striped suit, walks back to us. "This is a heck of a way for a grown man to make a living."

I manage a smile. I'll bet he says this at every trial. It's like a play to him. My confidence, what little I have, is slipping by the minute.

If he wins our case, it'll be a feather in his cap, nothing more. He wins so many cases, and this is just a day's work for him. For us, it's Laura's future.

The judge, smiling, announces that since we're still waiting, he will handle some other court affairs in his chambers. Two thin lawyers leave the courtroom with him.

I feel like screaming. I look up to the large clock on the greenish wall, lean over Laura and put my hand on Don's arm.

"This waiting is the worst."

"Yeah."

The bailiff comes out and says something to the clerk. The late juror, a man, comes running into the courtroom, up the aisle and into the jury room. But now the judge is gone. The reporters have given up taking pictures and stand in the back, talking. I wonder what would happen if I passed out.

The door to the judge's chambers opens and he strides in. His smile lights up his whole face. The twelve jurors file in and take their seats. No one is smiling. I know right away that we've lost. One of them would be smiling if we had won. I feel sick. How could they agree with the defense?

The clerk stands up. "Will the foreman please hand the verdict to the judge?"

The foreman, the man with the portable telephone, hands the verdict to the bailiff, who gives it to the judge.

The judge opens the verdict and starts to read silently, pen in hand. It looks like a term paper. I thought it would be just a note that had one or two words on it. He makes a few notations. He turns the page over carefully and sets it aside. He starts reading another page. His smile is gone. My heart is standing still. The movies I've seen must skip this part, because it's so boring. The judge is still on the second page. He writes more notes on the paper. He turns another page. He starts to write more. He hasn't smiled yet. We've lost. The judge has been smiling from the first day. I've never talked to him, but I always feel reassured that he's up there in control. I don't know if he's on our side or not, but he should be. He seems so kind and compassionate. Now there are no more smiles.

The judge finally hands the verdict to the clerk, his face impassive.

"Will the clerk please read the verdict?"

Oh, please hurry. I don't care anymore. I just want it to be over. I know we've lost. It makes me sick.

"Case #56-43 in the superior court of Orange County, Judge Francisco Firmat presiding."

Just say the verdict and get it over with. The clerk starts reading.

"Question number one." Oh no, she's going to read all the questions. All eighteen of them!

"Was Casper's Park in a dangerous condition on March 23, 1986? Answer yes or no. Answer. "Yes."

I'm squeezing Laura's hand. Oh, at least we have one in our favor. But what will it mean if all the rest are no's and we lose the case?

"Question number two. Was the dangerous condition in Casper's Park on March 23, 1986, caused by the county of Orange? Answer yes or no. Answer. "Yes."

Great. I squeeze Laura's hand again. That's two for us.

Question three comes back yes. How can they change now? It's beginning to look good, but I can't let myself think that we've won. Not yet.

We get more and more "yes" answers for each question.

"Question number 15. Was Sue Small negligent in the care of her daughter on March 23, 1986? Answer yes or no. Answer. "No.""

Somewhere deep inside me, I feel a huge wave of relief. All those years of people thinking I hadn't been watching Laura. I can't even count the times people had written letters, "But where was the mother when this happened?" No matter how many times I told the story, people couldn't believe that something terrible could happen if I had been watching her.

Finally, after five long years, the jury has confirmed what I knew from the beginning: that I had been right there, almost holding her hand.

I bounce back to the present.

"Question number seventeen. How much, if any, is awarded to Laura Small?"

"Answer. The sum of two million, seventy-six thousand dollars."

I squeeze Laura's hand, then hug her. I reach over to Don and hug him. We won. We won the case.

The moment is here and I can't even feel it inside. My stomach is still in knots, waiting for the verdict. It doesn't know yet that we've won. We won. We really won. My brain doesn't even realize it yet. The jurors still have to be polled. The clerk has to go through every question again, to see how many voted yes or no.

"Question one. How many voted yes. Twelve yes, No, zero."

Question 2. Another unanimous vote. Question three. Again unanimous.

Every single question, all the important facts I worried about so much in the trial-the location, the wilderness-all the jurors were unanimous in our favor. The jury got it. They believed Wylie instead of Barry Allen. It's over.

But no, now the judge starts talking. I try to listen to him, but I really don't care what he's saying. I really like him. But I don't want to listen to him. He tells us how important it is to have the jury system. We won! He thanks everyone for their time and patience and hard work on the jury. We just won the case! He goes on and on and my attention is completely gone. We won. I still can't feel anything inside. Laura sits politely next to me. She's listening attentively to the judge. I want to get out of this stifling courtroom.

I look over at Barry Allen, sitting at his table. I can see his face because he's turned sideways. He looks red and tight-lipped and disgusted. I don't care. I childishly hope he'll have a miserable weekend, the worst revenge I can think of in my euphoric mood.

The judge looks up and smiles at us for the first time as the jurors file out. Wylie and Rich walk back and we all shake hands. I have to tell my mom. So before I do anything else, I grab Laura by the hand and ask the bailiff if I can use the phone on her desk. My fingers shake as I call our home number.

"Hello?" I hear her hesitant voice.

"Mom. We won! We won the case!" Now we're both crying.

The courtroom is too loud, with many voices rising over mine.

"I'll talk to you later, ok? Tell David that we won." I hang up.

I hold Laura's hand and we walk back to Don.

"Are you ready?" he asks, and with Laura in between us, we walk out of the courtroom.

The cameras are whirring and the reporters explode with questions.

"How do you feel? What about the money? Was it less than you expected?"

How do I feel? The lawyers and visits to the courtroom, the horrible depositions, the testimony, the trial, the lawsuit; all of it had become a way of life. The constant worry had slipped into our days and nights. It was a bright orange thread woven into our lives, part of the fabric of every single day. Now it's been cut, abruptly.

My mind knows it's over, but the rest of my body is still living the last five years.

I smile and try to think fast. Microphones are in my face.

"We always believed the county was negligent and we're thrilled that the jury agreed with us."

What do I think about the money? I have no idea. I'm still trying to get it in my head that we won.

The reporters want Laura, and she steps up to a mike.

"What will you do with the money?"

"Pay medical bills, and go to college and stuff."

"What are you going to do now that the trial is over?"

"Go home," she replies with a smile.

"That's enough." I take her hand and we walk down the hall, followed by the cameras and reporters.

Credit: Los Angeles Times

I wish we could talk to the judge and jury. It's permitted, now that the trial is over, but I can't imagine turning around and going back down that reporter-infested corridor. We ride down the cramped mirrored elevator for the last time, and walk over to Wylie's office. I'm not excited enough. My mind knows we've won, but my stomach is still in knots.

As we walk out of the elevator into Wylie's office, his secretary is grinning widely. "Congratulations. We already heard it on the news."

That was fast. It's only been about ten minutes since the verdict was read. People I've never seen before pour out of doors to congratulate us. Everyone wants to hear the details. We wait for Wylie and Rich.

They walk in the door to cheers and laughter. Everyone is clapping. Wylie waves at us from across the room. He gets a call from the Associated Press and goes to his office to answer it.

Suddenly a wave of exhaustion hits me. The adrenaline must have run out, and I feel limp. All I want is to go home. We should talk to Wylie and thank him, or at least wait for him to come out of his office. Don and Laura and I stand around talking to the office staff for a few more minutes. I whisper to Don, "Let's get out of here."

He looks grateful as he nods in response. He takes Laura by the hand and we say goodbye and thank you. I tell Wylie's secretary to say goodbye to him and we walk out to the elevator. We say nothing for the short ride up to the parking garage roof. The August heat hits us, and the black car is sweltering as we climb inside. The air conditioner starts to work by the next block. I throw my red jacket on the back seat. Laura and I talk about silly things, Ebony the dog and Sylbuster the cat, about what David is doing right now, and the foreman of the jury and how we might see him at Disneyland sometime.

It feels good to let the "little things" flow back into my brain, like the tiny shells and debris left in a curving line by the receding tide. All the unimportant, the mundane, the bits and pieces of life that I've pushed away for so long. The worry is over. Life comes rushing back.

Don is smiling as we drive south on the Santa Ana freeway. The industrial buildings and train tracks look kind and comforting. I'm starting to smile inside.

Our nervous chatter has run out, and I sit watching the yellow center line rushing by in my vision. The pavement slips by, waves of heat rising from the concrete.

I think about my dad. Of everyone, he would be the least excited about our winning. It wouldn't matter to him. Money never meant anything to him. He would have been happy that I was happy. I wish he were still alive, but not like at the end. The way he used to be, laughing and telling his old stories of Germany. Other people will be glad for us. The waitress at the little grill by the courthouse. I wish I could tell her we won. My mom. Mike, of course. I wonder if he knows yet. It was his work that made this possible.

And my sisters. I'll call them as soon as we get home. Sid, and Dr. Watanabe and Dr. Palmer. We were so lucky to have the best doctors in Orange County; they saved her life. The prayer group at church; the people who brought months of dinners to us.

I smile at Laura and grab her hand as we pull onto our block. My mind forms the words, "Thank you, thank you," like a prayer, but I remember again that there is no God. Still, I want to thank someone.

Five years swirl in my mind. Wylie walking to the witness stand, wire-rimmed glasses in hand, ready to pounce on a witness. Don, tenderly removing the bandages from Laura's scarred head, his face impassive but his heart as raw as her wounds. Ebony climbing up on the couch with Laura and putting his head in her lap. David running for help. Endless Strawberry Shortcake movies with Laura. Watching her sleep at night, her arms around the yellow banana. The helicopter blades slicing through the sky, whipping the dead grass. The Angels games with Mike. Greg standing, branch in hand, as he tells me to pick up my baby. All these people, friends, doctors, strangers, heroes, family-they pulled Laura out of the lion's den. I thank them all, with all my heart.

Epilogue

2002

I see Laura at the door of the coffee shop. She struggles to open the door, balancing her schoolbooks and purse with her left hand. I wave, but she doesn't see me and goes straight to the counter. Her long black hair covers her face as she sets her books down and rummages through her purse for a few stray dollars.

I wave as she turns. Her face lights up. She gathers her books and walks to my table in the corner.

"Hi. Mom. Sorry I'm late," she says, breathless and excited. I stand and hug her across the table. I see the young businessman at the next table look away. He's been watching her since she came in.

Laura is stunning. She never dresses in regular school clothes. She dresses for an elegant affair, a tea perhaps on the lawn of a rich Orange County estate. Her white lace blouse looks cool in the summer heat, and the black beaded choker and earrings match her flowing black hair and set off her now flawless ivory skin. What a long way she's come since that morning in the park almost sixteen years ago.

She bubbles with excitement about her biology class. Anything about animals gets her talking. She's getting her pre-vet degree and wants to be the head of an animal shelter. The mountain lion is a distant memory.

Her worst fears, confessed one night as we sat in a restaurant booth with the family, were a space walk, and sharks.

"Not a mountain lion?"

"No. But I'm deathly afraid of sharks. Their eyes are so cold and unfeeling."

I'm glad she hasn't let fear of the mountain lion dictate her life. Her face is beautiful, no scars except a few faint lines easily covered by her ivory makeup. Her large contact fits over her right eye, beautifully matching her other eye.

She'll never be able to use her right hand. In all these years, I've never seen the fingers move or the wrist rotate. Laura calls it her decorative arm, good for holding large items. But she's learned to compensate, is a wonderful artist, and can do most anything she needs to do. She can give a cat a pill with only one hand, something I find impossible to do with two.

As we sit at the corner table, I pull out the tiny book of questions that David gave me for my birthday. It's called *4000 Questions to Ask Other People*. I love discovering things about people's lives; what people love and hate, what choices they would make, their favorite things.

As I sip my hot chocolate, Laura trying to find the mocha below the whipped cream, I flip through the pages for a new question.

I wish Don and Dave were here, but Dave's on tour with his band, somewhere near Niagara Falls, heading to Canada. Don's at work. His new optical company, started with two other friends, including Roger, has been quite successful in its first four years. Besides, he doesn't like to answer silly questions like these.

I laugh. "Here's an easy one. 'If you could go back and change one day in your life, which one would it be?' Well, I know what our answer would be."

Laura looks past me to the palm trees blowing outside.

"March 23rd, of course," I remind her.

She keeps looking out the window, pushing her long black hair from her face.

"Well, wouldn't that be the day you would change? Just think what a difference that would have made in our lives."

She puts down the mocha coffee. "No, that wouldn't be the day I would change. Not at all."

I stare at her.

"That day changed all of us, I know. But I wouldn't have become the person I am today, and we wouldn't have cared for each other as much as we do, or have such a wonderful family."

"But Laura, it was so horrible for you and those years of doctors and operations and…" I trail off, not knowing what else to say. Of course she knows. She was the one living through all of it.

"No, I would leave that day just like it was."

I look outside at the white clouds dotting the sky. The traffic crowds the intersection and, I hear a horn in the distance. I think maybe Laura is right. That fateful day made her the person she is today, and made all of us into different people. I hope that we have become better and kinder. My heart knows that we have, and I would never want to change that.

I smile at her and take another sip of the chocolate. "Ok, next question."

Acknowledgements

I am so grateful to all those people who helped save Laura's life that first day. Greg Ysais, who fought off the lion. Our son David, who ran for help. The firefighters and paramedics at San Juan Capistrano, as well as the helicopter pilots. The doctors at Mission Hospital, including Dr. Sylvain Palmer, neurosurgeon; Dr. Michael Shannon, pediatrician; Dr. Michael Kennedy, head of trauma; Dr. Michael Watanabe, plastic surgeon; and Dr. Sidney Weiss, pediatric ophthalmology. Without their excellence and dedication, Laura would not have lived. Later that year, Dr. Mitchell Cairo helped Laura with the diagnosis and treatment of aplastic anemia.

We are grateful to our friends who stayed with us that first long night, Cindy and Roger Johnston, Linda and Joe Gatlin, and our family doctor, Dr. John Coon and his wife.

We thank everyone who helped us those first few months; a community of strangers who came to our assistance, the nurses and staff at Mission Hospital, dinners every night from my choir friends, Easter baskets for the children, the banana, a friend who set up a trust fund. And all those people who contributed money and letters to a little girl they didn't know, from all over the country.

Laura's teacher, Miss Roberta, would visit every day with a new aid to help Laura regain her mobility, and bring toys and movies.

When we realized that the county might have known about the danger of a mountain lion attack, we called on Mike Madigan, friend and private investigator. He introduced us to Richard Staskus, our first lawyer, who took a chance with our difficult case. Thanks to all those who helped us with the investigation and trial, especially our trial lawyer, Wylie Aitken. Wylie's reputation as one of the best lawyers in America is based on an outstanding knowledge of his cases, as well as a brilliant performance in the courtroom. Thanks to his entire staff, especially Richard Cohn, his partner.

Thanks to all those reporters and journalists from the Los Angeles Times and the Orange County Register, especially Eric Lichtblau who covered the trial, and Vicki Vargas from NBC News.

Thank you to Jim Abbott, pitcher for the Angels, to care enough to write to a little girl he didn't know.

When I started writing the book, Laura's teacher Marcia Sargent, a published author, helped with publishing advice.

Another friend, Kathy Heckethorn, read many of the drafts and helped with the rewrites.

Many thanks to my editor, Lisa Leonard-Cook, who called late one night after reading the first chapter, because she couldn't wait till morning to find out what had happened to Laura. She was meticulous and brilliant as an editor and author, and will be missed.

My daughter-in-law, Heather Kelsey-Small, helped with the layout and formatting of the book, and endless encouragement.

Thanks to Dr. Paul Levesque, dean and former Chair of Religious Studies at California State University at Fullerton, for his encouragement, advice, and endless talks about atheism and religion.

My sisters, Jane Harper and Carol Bryan.

My son David, who has been patient, encouraging and loving all these years. I am so thankful he is our son.

And I thank my husband Don, for all the years of working hard to support his artistic, musical family in all our endeavors. And for his generosity and love during our forty-two years of marriage.

And my daughter Laura, who encouraged me every step of the way. I am so thankful for my family, and so lucky to have them.

Mr. David Wade, a wildlife artist, painted the cover picture. I was able to use it courtesy of Outdoor Life Magazine.

About the Author

Susan Mattern was born in St. Louis, MO. When she was eighteen, she joined the School Sisters of Notre Dame, a Catholic teaching order. She left after six years, still believing in God, but realizing the Catholic church might never change.

She moved to California to teach high school, and met her husband Don. They have two children, David and Laura.

Susan has taught creative writing, English, music, and religion in high school. She has also taught piano privately for many years, and was the music director at a large Catholic church. She and her husband are retired and live in Orange County. She still plays Bach, teaches ESL, and loves to write.

Please visit her website, outofthelionsden.net, for more information about the book.